The
Sacrament
of
Christian Life

The Sacrament of Christian Life

Mary Peter McGinty

THE THOMAS MORE PRESS
Chicago, Illinois

Excerpts of Scripture text used in this work are taken from *The Jerusalem Bible,* copyright 1966 by Doubleday & Company, Inc., Garden City, New York.

Excerpts from the documents of Vatican Council II are taken from *Vatican Council II: The Conciliar and Post Conciliar Documents,* copyright 1975 by Costello Publishing Company, Inc., and Reverend Austin Flannery, O.P.

ISBN 0-88347-270-8

CONTENTS

To my mother and my sister
who are grace for me

PREFACE

CHRISTIAN identity and practice are being seriously challenged by the rapid changes in American society. The diversity of cultures, beliefs and value systems merging into the experience of contemporary life call into question the validity and effectiveness of age-old traditions. This is particularly true for many Roman Catholics for whom the ritual actions of the sacraments have always formed a solid basis for belief. Modern life, with its dominant characteristics of pluralism and secularity, requires Christians to seek a renewed understanding of the reality of Christian faith and to make a new commitment to Christian living within a world of many visions. This book intends to focus on Christian living as the sacrament of the presence of the risen Jesus in today's world. For Catholic Christians, the ritual actions of the community of faith express and enable their living and, therefore, continue to provide a solid base for faith and life. The Spirit is at work in a community gathered to worship the Father, the Spirit who is sent to enlighten and encourage the faith of the disciples: "When the Spirit of truth comes, he will lead you to the complete truth . . . he will tell you of the things to come" (Jn 16: 13). It is hoped that this book will serve to clarify the meaning and importance of Christian living for the world and the significance of specific ritual sacramental actions in an ongoing struggle to carry out the mandate of Jesus: "I commissioned you to go out and to bear fruit, fruit that will last" (Jn 15: 16).

Throughout the text, my indebtedness to Bernard Cooke is obvious. Many colleagues, students, and friends have also contributed, knowingly or unknowingly, to the development of ideas expressed in these pages. Special gratitude is due to Frans Jozef van Beeck, S.J., who patiently and carefully read the entire manuscript and whose constructive criticisms are very much appreciated. My thanks to the editors, John Sprague and Joel Wells, for their expert guidance.

INTRODUCTION

I
N THE ordinary living experience in our contemporary society, Christian sacraments are becoming less important. This is especially obvious among Catholic Christians for whom sacraments have served traditionally as the basis of their faith life. At one time, Catholics could identify the larger community as at least nominally Christian, sharing certain beliefs and values while requiring at least a minimal conformity to specific Christian practices. Religious holidays were observed by all; Sunday was a day for church and family; children were expected to know the catechism; infants were baptized before they could be taken out to visit. Today, Catholics, along with other Christians, live in the midst of a pluralistic society which often favors neutrality in beliefs and values and encourages an indifference in practice. As a result, people have a tendency to live through everyday experiences without relating them to church. There is, in fact, not only a respect for separation of church and state but also a subtle promotion of separation of church and life.

In such an atmosphere, people are less likely to seek the Christian sacraments as meaningful actions in their lives. Instead, they begin to wonder why we have the sacraments at all; what a sacramental ritual adds to their daily life experience. Indeed, this is a very basic question. For, sacraments are not, and cannot be, isolated events. They are meant to be at the very center of Christian living. As such, they are expressive of, and conditioned by, a specific under-standing of human life, of Christian community, of Jesus Christ. It is no wonder, then, that Catholic sacramental prac-tice is somewhat confused. Not only does society confront the Christian faith with problems never faced before, but the human mind is coming up with faith understandings that open new ways of thinking and acting. Anthropology has presented new ways of viewing the human person in relation with self, others, and the world. The responsibility of the human per-son for the development of self and of the universe has been given new emphasis, leaving aside the tendency to praise or blame God for all that happens. New significance has been placed on the interrelatedness of all persons with each other and with the world in which they live, making it impossible for any one to live in isolation from the others. Christian faith can draw upon this knowledge to clarify the primary relation with God. Each person is loved by God, gifted with his love in order to live in communion with others in har-mony with the whole of the universe. But even within the context of the Christian faith there have been developments. Sacrament is understood in a much broader sense, to include any person or event or thing which manifests the presence of God in a way that makes his love touch human lives. Ec-clesiology has taken on whole new perspectives following the declarations of Vatican II. The council fathers identified the church as ''sacrament — a sign and instrument, that is, of

The Sacrament of Christian Life

communion with God and of unity among all men'' (LG 1). The sacrament of church is not a thing or an organization, but it is the people of God, a people who bear responsibility to and for the world. In like manner, studies in Christology have re-identified Jesus as truly divine and as truly human, fully human in risen life today. In his humanity, Jesus is sacrament, is effective presence of the divine love in our midst.

With the changes in living and the changes in knowledge, Christians are aware of the fact that the traditional understanding and the practice of the sacraments have become inadequate to deal with the problems of contemporary life. Continued performance of specific rituals which are said to cause certain effects when properly performed is not touching the lives of the people in readily observable ways. Big cities, which claim large numbers of Christian people, are the scenes of violence, crime, greed, exploitation, poverty, abuse, infidelity, apathy, and hostility of every kind. Where is the vital presence of that divine love which can bring life out of death and hope out of despair? It needs to be expressed in the lives of people who not only believe in a compassionate and caring God, but who live that faith in the moments of each day. Is it possible for a renewed understanding of sacramental life to make a difference? Yes, if people are willing to give it a chance. Jesus took the risk of touching people with that alluring love in all types of human situations. Christians, disciples of Jesus, are called upon and committed to letting that transforming love enter into the life of our world.

Mary Peter McGinty

The Meaning of Sacrament

This commitment may call for a shift in the understanding of sacrament and of the place of ritual in Christian life. For many Christians, the word sacrament calls to mind the formal ritual actions of the Church: eucharist, baptism, penance. For some, the word indicates an action which a priest performs on behalf of a person or group. A priest baptizes an infant who is thus freed from sin and identified as a Christian; a priest pronounces the words of absolution, bringing God's forgiveness into the life of the penitent; a priest pronounces the words of consecration which make Jesus present on the altar. People tend to identify the sacrament with the rite, with a specific moment of celebration. And this moment is often looked upon in a highly individualistic manner as a personal encounter of the believer with God: the infant cleansed from sin, the penitent restored to grace, the believer united with Jesus in communion. For some, God acts through the priest to establish or renew his relationship with this person, but this relationship is looked upon rather too much as a one-to-one, personal and private affair.

Such a view also tends to emphasize, not so much the fullness of the experience, as the correctness of what is done in order that the effect may be assured. In traditional teaching on the sacraments, the major facts to be learned dealt with the proper ''matter'' and ''form'' for a ''valid'' sacrament. Sacraments were often understood as rites to be technically performed according to specific criteria in order to earn sal-

The Sacrament of Christian Life

vific grace for the individual. In some ways, the correctly performed rite was seen as providing a guarantee of God's response to our actions: pour the water, say the words, and be assured that the infant is free from original sin. Historically, individuals have been known to regard the sacramental rituals in a somewhat magical way: properly performed, they inevitably produced grace.

This attitude was sometimes accompanied by a human approach to divinity that focused on placating angry gods or earning favor with powerful forces. For some Christians, salvation was in fact earned or bought by the performance of certain rituals: a baptized infant would go straight to heaven; one who received communion on nine consecutive First Fridays was assured of salvation; a penitent who performed a prescribed penance would escape punishment due to sin; a Christian who attended Sunday Mass was confident of being in the state of grace; a dying person who was anointed by a priest would surely enter into heaven. Thus the sacrament, identified with the rite, was meant to produce grace for the individual who was the object of the ritual action. This way of understanding sacraments gave priority to the individual who had to earn salvation. It emphasized the value and efficacy of the rite understood as a cause that guaranteed a certain effect. What happened was that the sacramental *life* of the church was effectively reduced to the sacramental *rituals*.

With Vatican II, the Christian community entered into a new phase in the sacramental expression of faith, an accep-

Mary Peter McGinty

tance of the loving God into the full reality of human life
and a recognition of a variety of ways in which that presence
of God is experienced in human lives. No longer can God
be relegated to the heavens, to be approached only through
designated mediators in specified ritual actions. The community is called to a contemporary expression of faith, an
authentic faith which has real connection with life as people
experience it. The documents of Vatican II open up new
understandings of church and of Christian life which challenge
the existing sacramental practice. The church is presented
as a people, an assembly of those who accept Jesus as Lord,
and are attentive to the Spirit of God acting in their midst;
a people who participate in and take responsibility for the
vitality of Christian life as a whole. Sacramental rituals are
viewed as actions of this assembled community within which
individuals have identity as disciples of Jesus and experience
the presence of the living God in those who know him;
wherein individuals and the community perceive the meaning of the situations in their human living in terms of the
gospel vision. The rituals consistently link up with daily experience in concrete lives, and Christian life becomes a way
of carrying out the mission of Jesus in the midst of everyday
occurrences. Jesus let the love of the Father touch the adult-
eress (Jn 8: 3-11), the taxgatherer (Lk 19: 1-10), the woman
with five husbands (Jn 4: 5-30), those with physical handicaps
(Mt 8: 1-17), the self-important pharisees (Jn 3: 1-21), the
oppressed and the abused (Mk 1: 40-42; Jn 5: 1-16). Christian life is meant to be what Jesus is: a sacrament of love

The Sacrament of Christian Life

reaching out to every person as an assurance of God's presence and concern.

One purpose of this book is to shift the primary focus on the sacramental life of the Church away from identification with and reliance on the seven ritual actions as means of salvation to recognition of the role of the daily living experience of the Christian people as the basic sacrament wherein this people functions as the body of Christ in the world. It is an attempt to identify sacramental rituals as specific expressions and enablers of the sacrament of Christian life. This is not a new idea. For the Israelites, ritual celebrated what God had done in their entire history and, more significantly, what God was still doing for them at the moment of celebration. The Christian ritual is meant to be such a moment of revelation, making present the entire love of God expressed in Jesus and, most importantly, celebrating the effectiveness of that love in the present moment.

For example, in the rite of eucharist, we remember the convenant God who cared for his people throughout the forty years in the desert (Ex 16: 35); the compassionate Jesus who would not send the people away hungry but multiplied loaves and fishes that they might eat (Mk 6: 30-44). And we are challenged to do likewise for those among us who are hungry and have no place to sleep, and to do so, not for recognition or reward, but simply as an expression of Christian love: this is what Jesus wants to do through his body, the church. To be a Christian involves a commitment to a total way of life, to the embodiment of a vision. It is a com-

17

mitment that needs to be, and can only be, lived out in the changing circumstances of everyday life. Adopting a Christ-like vision is the basis for a life of love, fidelity, reconciliation, forgiveness, service, acceptance; a life that is at once God-centered and other-centered. It is a challenge to love as God loves. "Love your enemies and pray for those who persecute you. . . . For if you love those who love you, what right have you to claim any credit? Even the tax collectors do as much, do they not? And if you save your greetings for your brothers, are you doing anything exceptional? Even the pagans do as much, do they not? You must therefore be perfect just as your heavenly Father is perfect" (Mt 5: 44-48).

The Church as Sacrament

The people of God, the church, is sacrament, "sign and instrument" (LG 1) of unity in God's love; in the daily living of the Christian people this sacrament is effective. Such an understanding does not detract from the importance of the *visible* gathering of the Christian people, nor from the efficacy of the communal *actions* of this body. It rather highlights the purpose of and the reason for the existence of the Church and the rituals: that the risen Jesus may be effectively present through his body the Church in order to reveal to all peoples the transforming love of God. The Christians of the first centuries did not "go to church," to "receive" the sacraments; they had a sense of being church when they gathered to celebrate the presence of the risen Lord. The

The Sacrament of Christian Life

disciples of Jesus, in the church of Jerusalem, "remained faithful to the teaching of the apostles, to the brotherhood, to the breaking of bread and to the prayers. . . . The faithful all lived together and owned everything in common. . . . They went as a body to the Temple every day but met in their houses for the breaking of bread; they shared their food gladly and generously; they praised God and were looked up to by everyone" (Acts 2: 42-47).

The Christian people need to be conscious of the presence of the risen Lord in their ordinary life experiences and thus enable Jesus' offer of life to reach out to the wider community of God's people. The Church is meant to be a proclamation of and a revelation of God's love for the world. It is a love that speaks within human experience, in a secular context, with an invitation to live a full human life. Christian life can function within the world as an embodiment of that love, to support and challenge the meaning of everyday events; to discover the meaning in each life and to offer the possibility for communion. Only then will the mission of Jesus, to make the Father known and loved, be realized. The people in our cities are faced with a paradox: they value a certain personal anonymity and yet have a deep-seated desire for communion. Youngsters instinctively guard their individuality, yet want to be "one of the crowd." The love expressed in Jesus respects the autonomy of the individual and yet invites each one into a personal relation of union. Somehow, therefore, the community which identifies itself as the body of Jesus

19

Mary Peter McGinty

must allow that love to reach all people, and especially the persons most in need.

Organization of this Book

The order in which the rites will be discussed is different from the traditional presentation which moves from baptism to the final anointing. The reason for the change in order lies in an emphasis on daily living, a focus on the concrete experience of life for mature Christians. Eucharist and marriage are the core experiences of everyday Christian life, while reconciliation and anointing come into play at specific moments to heal and comfort and renew the life of the whole body. Ministry is always operative to keep the body functioning. Initiation rites are the way to enter into the church, beginning the process of Christian life for individuals and keeping the community mindful of its Christian identity and purpose. Again, the focus is meant to shift from the rituals to the basic sacrament of Christian life, to the people who make the risen Jesus effectively present in the world as it is.

The material in this book is ordered in a way that seeks to clarify and support the stated purpose of identifying the whole of Christian living as sacramental. A first section deals with a renewed understanding of what is meant by the sacramental life of the Church, and the context within which such a view can be developed. Contemporary thought has introduced major shifts in our thinking: the way we approach God through human symbols which need to be alive in order to be meaningful and effective; our knowledge of human life

20

The Sacrament of Christian Life

in this world with its plurality of cultures, social classes and generations; the encounter through word and action with a Jesus who is thoroughly human, who is risen, and who is divine; a renewed sense of belonging to and of responsibility for the community called Church and for the world it is intended to serve.

A second section deals with those actions of the assembled Christian community which express the mature reality of commitment to Christ and challenge the living out of that commitment. For being Christian is not just an individual endeavor, but it relies upon the cooperative efforts of the whole body of Christ to respond to the action of the Spirit in our midst. The initiative of God's love is embodied in Jesus whose presence is celebrated in the Christian rites. The basic rituals which support and prompt the daily living of the Christian people are those of eucharist and marriage, for a people who seek to live in response to God's gift of love and in life-giving union with one another.

The eucharistic liturgy serves to recognize the marvelous works of God in our midst and to praise the intensity of God's love expressed in the death and resurrection of Jesus. The liturgy spells out the gospel message of discipleship; it challenges the Christian community and the individual Christian to see the ordinary events of life as opportunities to receive the gifts of a loving God and to be a true body of Christ for others. It brings to light the dependence of Christ on his body to provide the human experience of his love for the people of this world. It focuses on the fidelity of God

21

to his people and thus encourages gratitude for goodness in life and hope in difficulties. The eucharistic liturgy is meant to gather in the life experience of this assembled people, offer it to God in union with Christ's experience of human life, ponder it within the context of the fidelity of God's love, awaken gratitude for all that has been, and challenge the community to bring the full impact of this love into the concrete events of daily life.

The union of two persons in marriage introduces a Christian couple into a specific way of living this vision. Their commitment, made explicit in the rite of matrimony, is an embodiment of the relation of God with his people, and more specifically, of the relation of Christ with his body, the Church. Within the Christian community, the married couple serves as a powerful sacrament of the unconditional love and fidelity which bring about union and new life. This way of living is a challenge which needs to be worked out in all the details of everyday life. It is a lifestyle which is possible only with the support of a believing community, and which cannot grow without an involvement in the wider world context. This Christian sacrament functions within the family, within the Church, and within the world on a daily basis.

While eucharist and marriage are basic rituals of life and growth in life for the Christian community, other rituals play significant roles and address specific needs of the body. Among the traditional sacramental rites are two which bring healing and wholeness to the body so that it may function well. Reconciliation is an ongoing process of acceptance and

The Sacrament of Christian Life

forgiveness. Human life inevitably involves conflict and irresponsible action; at times, it involves malice and hatred. The need for reconciliation is constant. Christians who can accept the fidelity of God's love are able to extend their experience of forgiveness into their own life situations and further the healing process of the whole. Thus, the sacramental presence of the love of God enters into the daily life experiences of the world. Fidelity and forgiveness, expressed and shared in the communal rite of reconciliation, become operative in society.

The healing of the incapacities brought on by illness or aging is another of the sacramental functions of the Christian community. Those who feel weak and useless need to feel the touch of that love which supports their living and gives value to their continuing presence. In the ritual of the anointing of the sick, a Christian community can touch the sick person with the compassion and encouragement of God's love, expressing its willingness to provide needed assistance in meeting the challenge of drastically changed circumstances which are encountered every day. Again, that body of Christ is called upon to function sacramentally on behalf of those in need.

In addition to concern for the wholeness of the body, the community is aware of the need for leadership and service if the parts of the body are to function effectively. The Christian community, assembled as a body, or interspersed as leaven throughout the society, has concrete needs to be ministered to by those of its members who are specifically called to such service. In the rituals of ordination and commissioning, the community designates ministers to act on its behalf and for its benefit in various ways. These ministers are intended to embody the love of God for his people in the service they render. They fulfill the role of disciple of Jesus in a visible way and enable the whole body to function more effectively.

But this body cannot be presumed or taken for granted. No one is born a Christian. The body exists because of deliberate decision on the part of those who choose to become disciples of Jesus Christ, or of those who commit themselves to live in such a way that their children will grow up as Christians. The specific ways of living as a Christian, of being Church, of being the body of Christ, of being sacrament of God's love are the daily implementations of a commitment which is made explicitly in the initiation rites of baptism, confirmation, and eucharist. Introduction into the Christian way of life entails a process of awareness and decision, a sense of belonging and responsibility. Becoming a Christian is a lifelong task which culminates in the entry into risen life. Yet, it is that decision to begin, expressed in the rituals of initiation, which underlies the reality of a sacramental life, a life whose goal is the realization of the kingdom of a loving God.

A final section of the book projects possibilities for the life of the Christian community in the light of present challenges and opportunities. The world is new each day. New insights are constantly opening up new vistas for us in

The Sacrament of Christian Life

our experience of human life and of our Christian faith. The Church has entered into a new phase of existence, with circumstances and situations never encountered before. This is nothing unexpected, for the Christian vision has come through many centuries of change. From the early experience of being church, Christians moved into a second phase of a technical defining of rites. The present phase of renewal seeks to relate ordinary life experience to the event of Jesus through community liturgical actions. Now the gospel vision must address the life experience of a new people in a new world setting. The reality of today's world with its unique characteristics needs to be a critical force in seeking meaning for Christian life as an effective and valid expression of God's love. Through it all, the fidelity of God's love, embodied in the humanity of Jesus, enables and challenges the progress of his people in the building of the kingdom.

THE CHURCH'S LIFE
AS SACRAMENTAL

TO SAY that the sacramental life of the Church is encountered in the daily living of the Christian people may sound strange to some who are accustomed to thinking of sacrament as a specific ritual action of the gathered Christian community. Few Christians are likely to apply the word directly to themselves. Yet, when we look to Jesus as our guide, we find that he entered the human world to make his Father known to all and he did this primarily by his living amongst us. "To have seen me is to have seen the Father. . . . The words I say to you I do not speak as from myself: it is the Father, living in me, who is doing this work" (Jn 14: 9-10). He became what we are, as the incarnation of the boundless reality that is God. He is the embodied presence of God in our midst. Jesus is the human way of being God who reveals the love God has for us in terms we can understand. He puts us in touch with God by his own human living through days and months and years of human history. Our own sacramental experience can have meaning only in the perspective of Jesus as sacrament of the Father's love.

The Humanity of God: Jesus and Church

It was God's initiative, so typical of the divine sensitivity to our needs, to reveal himself to us in Jesus. Due to human limitations, if people are to know the God who is love, they

The Sacrament of Christian Life

need to experience him in their own lives — they need to meet *witnesses,* persons who express and embody the love that is God. Jesus, in his humanity, gives us *the* authentic human expression of who God is. "If you know me, you know my Father too" (Jn 14: 7). In his human encounters on earth, Jesus revealed to everyone he met the goodness and the challenge of the Father's love as it touched their own particular lives. Countless examples come to mind: the healing of the man born blind, the restoration of dignity to the woman taken in adultery, the conversion of the woman at the well, the reconciliation with the thief on the cross. Each felt loved, each was transformed in the acceptance of that love, and each was challenged to live the new life.

Now that he is risen, untouchable and untouching (or rather, touching more deeply in the Spirit), Jesus asks no less of us his followers than what he himself achieved — to be the embodiment, the sacrament of divine love wherever we are: healing illness, reconciling conflicts, challenging indifference, forgiving offenses, embracing those most in need of love. He asks us to be his body, the sacrament of his presence, allowing him to continue his mission to all God's people. "Father, may they be one in us, as you are in me and I am in you" (Jn 17: 21). Jesus is sacrament of the Father; the community of believers is sacrament of the risen Jesus. It is in this context that Christian living in this world takes on significance and meaning as truly sacramental — tangible experience of a love that is faithful and unconditional. Ritual actions of the assembled body are sacrament in so far as they gather up and express this lived experience of the marvelous acts of God within the lives of his people. The link between life and ritual is essential for the effectiveness of the ritual.

Vatican II took a good look at the community called church and identified it as the concrete form of God's action in this world, "a living witness to him, especially by a life of faith and love" (LG 12). The people of God, as the embodiment of divine love, are called to active participation in the mission of Jesus. "They should everywhere on earth bear witness to Christ" (LG 10). Responding to this call is a task which is lived out in the hourly, minute-by-minute experience within a particular culture and social setting. The unity of the church demands that its presence be different wherever it is, just as the one Jesus responded differently to those around him. With the sinner, he was compassionate: "Your faith has saved you; go in peace" (Lk 7: 50). Jesus treated Peter with praise and confidence, "You are Peter and on this rock I will build my church" (Mt 16: 18), yet cautioned him against weakness, "Get behind me, Satan! Because the way you think is not God's way but man's" (Mk 8: 33). Jesus was sensitive to the needs of the crowds, "I feel sorry for all these people; they have been with me for three days now and have nothing to eat. I do not want to send them off hungry" (Mt 15: 32). Yet he was strong in warning against the lure of wealth, "How hard it is for those who have riches to enter the kingdom of God" (Mk 10: 23-24). Jesus sat at table with tax collectors and accepted the hospitality of pharisees, yet

The Sacrament of Christian Life

openly spoke against their hypocrisy and their abuse of the people. In every situation he encountered, Jesus made the love of the Father an active force to be reckoned with.

In our world today, the mission of Jesus involves a wide diversity of expressions. There is no standard way to be body of Christ, to be church, to be sacrament in the world. The underlying question is always, "How would Jesus see this situation?" or "How is God to be present here?" The challenge is to be that kind of presence toward each person we meet. Do we know a person who is hopelessly ill? Are we acquainted with people whom we label as sinners: adulterers, white-collar thieves, bigots, embezzlers? Are there people who obviously need help: abandoned children, the elderly, the addicted, the uneducated and unskilled? How are the people around us coping with stress, overwork, alienation, confusion? What does it mean to be sacrament of God's love in the society we live in? To be live parts of the body of Christ we must be human beings, active in building the world. So much that we are and do and suffer is dictated by the social and cultural customs of the place and the time in which we live; it takes real sensitivity and creative effort to draw attention to new possibilities opened up by the presence of a loving God. The embodiment of genuine love is needed to bring about effective change in a family gathering, a situation of illness or debilitating old age, a corporate board meeting, a demonstration for nuclear disarmament, a campaign for political power. The security of being loved is essential, and that love needs to be humanly expressed, sacramentally lived, in the famines of Africa, the oppression of the landless in Latin America, the conflicts in the Middle East, the emerging freedom in Eastern Europe, the dire poverty of Cairo and Calcutta, the repression in China, the wealth of Tokyo, Singapore, and Hong Kong. Each situation calls for a highly sensitive and responsible way of being there, of revealing the intensity and the power of Jesus' promise, "I am with you always" (Mt 28: 20).

A Community of Faith

For the Christian, the meaning of human living is expressed in and derived from the ritual actions of a community of faith which embraces the individual and to which the person has chosen to belong. Vatican II clearly states the impact of the ritual actions on the community: "The liturgy daily builds up those who are in the Church, making of them a holy temple of the Lord, a dwelling-place for God in the Spirit, to the mature measure of the fullness of Christ" (SC 2). A community of persons whose life is for the glory of God and who thus live in and for the world draws its strength and purpose from the risen Lord. "It is through the liturgy, especially, that the faithful are enabled to express in their lives and manifest to others the mystery of Christ" (SC 2). The ritual actions of the faith assembly are peak moments which come out of the lived experience of this community and feed into the effectiveness of that living. All of us learn of God and of Jesus, the sacrament of God's presence, from those who know them — "know" in a biblical sense — by having lived

The Sacrament of Christian Life

with them. The Christian community is precisely a gathering of the people who know Jesus as Lord. It is Jesus who draws them together. It is Jesus who is the root of their commitment. It is the risen Jesus whom they embody in this world. To know Jesus is to know the Father who sent him. Those who encounter this community of faith, this people gathered in his name, are put in touch with the Jesus who is its life. Within this community Jesus lives and has continued to live throughout the centuries. His way of life is the source of life for his disciples. His mission — to make God's love for his people known to all — is the bond which unites a disparate people and gives them identity and a name within the world. And it is Jesus, his way of life, his mission, that draws the Christian people together to praise the goodness and fidelity of the Father, to thank him for the risen Lord and his Spirit who make sense out of human existence, and to be immersed in the security and the challenge of that divine love. "The renewal in the Eucharist of the covenant between the Lord and man draws the faithful and sets them aflame with Christ's insistent love" (SC 10).

Together, in assembly and in ritual action, Christians seek out the meaning in their particular lives of the revelation to be found in the life and words of Jesus. Remembering all that God has done for and with his people, and most especially in the event of Jesus, the Christian community faces the challenge of letting this God enter effectively into its present world. Each day the people renew the commitment to be his body — hands and feet, eyes and ears and tongue —

31

so that all people can become aware of his presence in their lives.

God is Love

Such an understanding of sacramental life relies on a familiarity with God as the God who loves. In human history, it has been and continues to be a struggle to retain an image of God as good and loving. At times, God has been presented as one who rewards, but also punishes. Fear of punishment, especially in the form of a hell that never ends, sometimes leads Christians to seek ways of winning the favor of God. God is seen as a kind of scorekeeper, who tallies the good and the bad in each person's behavior and demands that the account be balanced. This can lead to a somewhat pagan practice on the part of some Christians who try to placate an angry God with prayers and promises, and try to make up for faults and deficiencies by self-inflicted denials and discipline. In the history of Christianity, reflections of this view of a god who seeks justice and retribution may be seen in the theory of the salvation of humanity by a ransom paid to a mercilessly demanding God with Jesus' suffering and death, and in the nervous gaining of indulgences as a way to diminish the punishment due to sin. For some Christians, such a view of God has caused them to live in a perpetual state of guilt, never sure that the account is balanced. For others, the tendency has been simply to give up the effort to balance the books, declare oneself worthless, and abandon any attempt at relationship with God. In the first case, some Christians see the

The Sacrament of Christian Life

sacramental rites as opportunities to gain points on the positive side, to balance out the account. Some will seek to overcome feelings of guilt by regularity in ritual practice. Attendance at Mass, completion of novenas, faithful recitation of fixed sets of prayers may become objectives in themselves. In the second case, some Christians simply cease all participation in the life of the Church, seeing it as a waste of time for one who is already lost. Without a sense of the fidelity of God's love for his people, the individual loses sight of the significance of belonging. Unfortunately, the Christian community may have played a role in fostering these images of God with the enumeration of penalties for certain sins and the encouragement of paying off the debt through good works and prayers. The whole system of earning merits falls within this perception. If one had to believe certain traditional expositions of the Catholic faith, to deliberately eat meat on Friday or to willfully miss Mass on Sunday merited the same penalty as murder or blasphemy: eternal punishment in hell.

Yet, the reality of God is so different from any arbitrary, demanding, vengeful, unforgiving image. As the Scriptures constantly remind us, God is a loving God, "a God of tenderness and compassion, slow to anger, rich in kindness and faithfulness" (Ex 34: 6-7); steadfast in all situations, ever present for his people, "Yahweh encircles his people now and for always" (Ps 125: 2). He does not exclude anyone from his love, nor set any conditions on the availability of that love. Rather, he loves with such an intensity that he actually chooses to become what we are and to dwell in our

33

midst, "The Word was made flesh, he lived among us, and we saw his glory" (Jn 1: 14). His total otherness and his shared humanness, his utter uniqueness and his concerned closeness are the mystery of our God.

Creation: A Love Process

This God who loves chooses to create a world as an expression of his uniqueness and his closeness. In other words, we live in a sacramental universe. God's relation with this world is creative, dynamic, and historical. His love continues to issue forth in myriads of possibilities. The vast universe is constantly involved in a creative process in which the interrelatedness and interdependence of all the parts is becoming increasingly clear to human intelligence, not only in our experiences on earth but most recently in human exploration of space.

It is also becoming increasingly clear that God does not dominate and manipulate the process, even when we think it might be to the advantage of the process. The creativity which is characteristic of love includes a freedom for the other to be itself and to work out its destiny within its own power and possibility. This does not mean an indifference or a withdrawal from the vitality of the process. Rather, God's presence to all that is provides a spark, a support, a stimulation, an assurance that what is possible can actually be. Love cannot remain apart from what is loved; its presence is powerful. Yet, it is characteristic of love not to interfere by force, but to respect the autonomy of what is loved. This God does

The Sacrament of Christian Life

for the world. Historically, in all the events since the beginning of time, God has been involved intimately in all that happens, not determining the outcome but injecting the pervasive power of intimate concern.

The Human Capacity for Love

All the characteristics of God's love for the universe of creation are especially capable of expression in the human person who is "created in the image of God," and to whom the world is given in stewardship. New insights developed by anthropology have led us to consider again the kind of relation humanity has to God and to the universe. Respect for the uniqueness and the autonomy of the human person and realization of an invitation to live in a communion of love give a different perspective on the human role in history. Can human beings be asked to assume the role of purely passive recipients of divine favors in a preordained universe? Or can persons be required to earn salvation, for which they are created, merely by the right combination of beliefs and actions? Is there not, rather, a call to enter into a dynamic, creative, cooperative effort of discovery, building, fulfillment? And, within that process, does God not truly need the sacrament of human expression to maintain a credible presence of his fidelity in love?

The human person has the ability to embody the reality of God in a way that is unique among all creatures: the capacity for self-forgetful love. A person can provide for others the experience of a love that asks no questions, places no

35

Mary Peter McGinty

demands, expects no returns; an experience of God. A person can enter into relationships which seek the good of the other, which respect the uniqueness of the other, which search for a unity which emphasizes their difference; an experience of God. God loves us intimately and personally, is concerned for our well-being, and respects our uniqueness. He expects us to be what we are: images of God, human embodiments of who he is. That makes us responsible for each other and for all of our world, to be the tangible expressions of God's love and presence. In fact, God depends on us for the human expressions that provide experience of his concern, for the human actions that bring awareness of and response to possibilities. He asks us to love what he loves and to care for it as he cares. He asks us, in our living, to be sacraments of his presence.

Jesus: *The* Sacrament of Love

Thus, the intensity of God's love is most fully expressed in God's becoming what we are: human. The full reality of God is humanly expressed in Jesus of Nazareth. He is *the* sacrament of divine love. What an incomprehensible thought: that God who is totally other would come into human history as one of us! That God who is love, who enjoys the dynamic unity of triune life, would enter into the incompleteness, the disruption, the limitation, the uncertainty of human experience. That God who is reality would know what it is to think humanly, to choose, to decide, to be accepted, to be rejected, to grow and to change, to learn and to discover;

The Sacrament of Christian Life

to experience in person what it is to be human and to live in this world. In his encounters with people, Jesus reveals both who God is and what it really means to be human. In the ordinary life of Jesus of Nazareth, people had an opportunity to know the God who is present to us. In every instance of his relatively short life, Jesus made the Father known to those he touched. "To have seen me is to have seen the Father" (Jn 14: 9). We can only wonder at the fact that God chose to live among us for thirty years in the ordinariness of an obscure village, helping with the daily chores, bringing water from the well, celebrating the festivals. "The child grew to maturity, and he was filled with wisdom" (Lk 2: 40). How precious ordinary living must be! Indeed, God is with us in all those moments that we tend to overlook — waking up in the morning, shopping for the groceries, mowing the lawn — in the obscurity and boredom of everyday events. And each of us has the opportunity to make God's love known to the storeclerk, the postman, the neighborhood children, even to one's co-workers and colleagues.

Love Made Present in Life

Jesus passes on this task to his disciples and, in a special way, to his visible body, the Church. "Established by Christ as a communion of life, love and truth, it is taken up by him also as the instrument for the salvation of all . . . it is sent forth into the whole world" (LG 9). It is this body that must present the newness of the vision, the newness of the approach to the situations in human life that is called for in a new social and cultural context. The Christian community embraces those who know the Lord Jesus, risen yet still among us. A people who have committed themselves to be his human presence in the world must assume the responsibilities of creative love. As a visible body, the Christian people continue the mission of Jesus: that all peoples may be united; that all of creation may be brought to fulfillment. As a human race, we crave a unity which seems to elude us constantly. As one part of the world begins to come together, another falls apart: Europe moves toward greater cooperation as the Middle East erupts in hostile confrontation. To become one world and one people requires the full power of love: "I give you a new commandment: love one another; just as I have loved you, you also must love one another" (Jn 13: 34) — with a love that is constant, faithful, and, in the last resort, unconditional. The Christian community has committed itself to be the effective embodiment of the risen Jesus to and for the world — a sacrament of the love of God, "a sign and instrument, that is, of communion with God and of unity among all men" (LG 1). The community of faith is meant to be a place where everyone is welcomed, where no one is rejected, where the sense of belonging is strong and the concern for one another is obvious. The Christian people are meant to be a presence that is always felt, that can be counted on, that does not succumb to fatigue or pressure, that does not avoid conflict but continues to love in the midst of adversity. In a word, the Church

The Sacrament of Christian Life

is meant to be Jesus, humanly living through this particular situation on this particular day.

The Necessity of Rituals

When we emphasize so strongly the sacramentality of the ordinary living of the Christian community and of the individual Christian, are we deemphasizing the importance of the rituals we commonly call sacraments? Far from it! Yet it is to be remembered that the sacraments do not exist in themselves; they are actions of Jesus, of his body the church, of a human community of believers. The sacraments, numbered seven, are critical actions of this community of Christians. They are moments in which the community assembles to express its faith, to share its lived experience of the risen Lord, to touch its tradition as a people, to renew its vision, to gain significance and meaning for what is presently happening in its life. Sacraments are meant to critique our lives as Christians. The main role of sacramental actions within the community is to recognize and praise the presence of the living God in our midst and to make that presence operative in the entire everyday life of the people. Without these moments, the community would cease to exist as an effective body, and the unity of life rooted in the one Lord would soon dissipate.

From the beginning, the disciples of Jesus gathered together to share and to support their experience of the risen Lord. They "met in their houses for the breaking of bread; they shared their food gladly and generously; they praised God and were looked up to by everyone'' (Ac 2: 46-7). The frequent gatherings took on the structure of the Jewish meal which marvelled at the action of God in the midst of his people, and of the Last Supper experience which interpreted that action in terms of Jesus. ''This is my body which will be given for you. . . . This cup is the new covenant in my blood'' (Lk 22: 19-20). In these gatherings, the early Christians could find meaning for the events of their lives, not only in the history of their relationship with the God of their fathers, but especially in the understanding of the Abba of Jesus. The ritual for these meetings developed around the proclamation of the word of God and the experience through symbolic action of the life, death, and resurrection of the Word become flesh. This ritual was and is the peak experience of Christian life, ''a sacrament of love, a sign of unity, a bond of charity'' (SC 47). It has endured throughout the centuries in the forms of the eucharistic liturgy which is the source of all sacramental living.

Around this ritual and interconnected with it, other rites came into being to help the community deal with the meaning of its life. ''The liturgy of the sacraments and sacramentals sanctifies almost every event of their lives with the divine grace which flows from the paschal mystery'' (SC 61). The community came to recognize the sacramentality of the union of man and wife in marriage, a union Paul identifies as symbol of the union of Christ and his Church. The meaning of God's love with its unconditional gift of self, its orientation to the

The Sacrament of Christian Life

other, its respect for the uniqueness of the other is most clearly and fully expressed in the human relationship of marriage. The ritual action in which the community could celebrate this paradigm of love, thus recognizing the sacramentality of this lived relationship in its midst, was slow in developing, but can be a powerful experience of life and a challenge to show forth the reality of love in a particular setting.

The whole problem of evil, whether it takes the form of suffering caused by sin or by physical weakness or both, can be brought into focus and assume some meaning when it is immersed in the experience of God's fidelity and concern. The community gathered in reconciliation and forgiveness provides a powerful antidote to the ravages of sin. So does the community that demonstrates its compassion assuage the fear and despair that accompany illness and death. The external rituals for healing within the community have changed over the centuries in a constant attempt to express the reality of God's love in very difficult human situations.

On another level, the members of the community are called upon to serve one another. Initially, Christians recognized the need to use their individual talents to further the effectiveness of the life of the body. They held themselves responsible for the life of the whole. Thus, there existed a wide variety of ministries according to the needs of the particular community. "To some this gift was that they should be apostles; to some, prophets; to some, evangelists; to some pastors and teachers; so that the saints together make a unity in the work of service, building up the body of Christ" (Ep 4:

Mary Peter McGinty

11-12). And there was a common practice of designating leaders who would preserve apostolic identity and authority in the community, and who would assume specific roles to be performed for and on behalf of the community. "Appoint elders in every town. . . . Since, as president, he will be God's representative, he must be irreproachable . . . a man who is hospitable and a friend of all that is good . . . and he must have a firm grasp of the unchanging message of the tradition" (Tt 1: 6-9). The rituals for the commissioning of various ministers specified the commitment to service that every Christian makes at baptism.

Not at all slow in coming about were the rituals for the initiation of new members into the visible body of Christians. The rites for catechumens, for baptism, and for confirmation date back to the early centuries of Christian life. They still provide a significant moment for stimulation and growth in the lives of the members, as well as a beginning of a way of life for the individual who is touched by this community action. For, each ritual is precisely that, an action of the community gathered to share its life and faith with an individual member in a way designated by the symbols of the rite.

The Context of Daily Life

Sacramental rituals are also intimately linked with the daily human experience of a people which is focused, challenged, and shared in these communal actions. Symbolic actions depend on the context for their significance. For the Christian community, the daily lives of the members provide the im-

The Sacrament of Christian Life

mediate context. Since Christianity is basically a way of life, the many and varied events of daily living are the reality of being Christian, the way in which the body of Christ actually functions. Within the context of everyday events, the Christian people can be sacrament of God's presence, can let his love be felt and his concern be evident. As the community gathers for ritual expression of its faith, the diversity of experience is brought together. From the beginning, unsurpassable boundaries were surpassed: ''all baptised in Christ, you have all clothed yourselves in Christ, and there are no more distinctions between Jew and Greek, slave and free, male and female, but all are one in Christ Jesus'' (Ga 3: 27-8). In today's community, teachers, parents, football teams, stockbrokers, storeclerks, nurses, and unemployed laborers assemble as one people. The meaning of events in their lives becomes clearer as they are placed in the context of the life and death experience of Jesus. This Christian people is challenged to approach the difficulties of life in this world as Jesus faced the situations in his life, with utter trust in the fidelity of God: ''it is the Father, living in me, who is doing this work'' (Jn 14: 10). In the assembly of believers, the joy and the sadness, the success and the failure of daily living can be shared and appreciated. And God can be known.

Apart from this context of daily experience, the sacramental actions can lose their efficacy and their meaning. They can become weak or empty symbols which people either abandon as useless or perform automatically in the vague hope of some type of reward. If people do not relate the story of

Mary Peter McGinty

Jesus' rejection by his people to their own experience of being ignored and passed over, then the word proclaimed in the ritual action has fallen on deaf ears and will not bring new possibility to that life. When people fail to connect the resurrection experience of Jesus with the ordinariness of their own lives, they also fail to understand the creative possibilities in suffering and the ultimate meaning of life. Symbols and rituals cannot, of themselves, create meaning and stimulate action. Rather, they rely on the total experience of the people who participate in these symbolic actions to give meaning and effectiveness to these signs. They are ways of remembering, communicating, and creating the meaning of life for this community.

Likewise, the daily living experience of the community derives its effectiveness and its meaning from the communal experience of the ritual sacramental acts. Human life has a long history and a variety of cultural expressions. This is true also of the Christian life. Within all this diversity, the individual needs to learn from others how to live. The family is the first and most important community within which the human person matures. Families come together in the community of faith to join with others in the attempt to live the message and mission of Jesus in a conscious and decisive way. And the community reaches out to the larger society to pursue the goal of unity of all peoples. The continuing focus of the gospel vision in repeated ritual experiences keeps the Christian people alert to the concerns of Jesus for the salvation of every person, and to the unconditional character

The Sacrament of Christian Life

of the love that can change the world. It is that love that can touch the hopeless, the abandoned, the frightened, the self-sufficient, the indifferent. It is that love which forms the Christian community in the celebration of sacramental rituals and spills out into all the areas of their lives.

Thus, the body of Christ is always *becoming*. For the Christian, the body of Christ is the revealer of Jesus Christ and his significance for human living. The community of believers embodies and celebrates the presence of God in the world. Through faithful participation in the life of the community and in the communal acts of worship, the individual is brought in touch with the loving, healing, caring, challenging God who can make sense out of the confusion of daily life. It becomes easier to be sensitive to the needs of others, to alleviate suffering where possible, to refuse success at the expense of others, to forgive wrongs yet refuse to accept evil in any form. To live as a Christian is not an individual task, to be achieved by self-mastery. To live as Christians is the call of a people, who need each other and the assembly of the whole to embody the compelling presence of that God who continues to demand while he continues to support.

For, sacrament is not something that is done to us, but something we become in the acceptance of Jesus as the living presence of God's love. ''You are a chosen race, a royal priesthood, a consecrated nation, a people set apart to sing the praises of God who called you out of the darkness into his wonderful light. Once you were not a people at all and now you are the People of God'' (1P 2: 9-10). Sacrament

Mary Peter McGinty

is a visible, tangible expression of who God is and how he relates with his people. Jesus in his human living so well expressed God's love, touching so many people with his healing, caring presence. The response was sometimes startling, sometimes hostile. But the presence was felt. Each Christian assumes the same mission at baptism: to make God known, to be an effective embodiment of his love, a sacrament of his presence. It takes a lifetime to approach that goal. The actual living in the ordinary and special situations of each day is the place where this sacramental action happens. At times, it is the action of the assembled community that puts God before the consciousness of the world. More often, it is in the unnoticed activity of the individual Christian in the common dealings with others — answering a phone call, greeting a friend, caring for the sick and the elderly, teaching the young, making corporate decisions, building homes, feeding and clothing the poor, defending the weak, resisting the lure of money, power, prestige, gathering for Bible study and mutual encouragement, helping young couples prepare for marriage — where the healing, caring love of God makes a difference. Here is the sacrament that expresses who God is and allows his presence to be felt, to be effective. Here is the expressive and effective sacrament of Christian living.

THE SACRAMENTS OF DAILY LIVING

EUCHARIST

EUCHARIST is the primary sacramental action of the Christian community. Christians can be characterized as a eucharistic people, not because they celebrate a ritual action called Eucharist, but because they live a way of life which is basically a form of praise and thanksgiving. St. Paul attempted to make it clear to the early Christians that worship involves more than offering ritual sacrifices. "Think of God's mercy, my brothers, and worship him, I beg you, in a way that is worthy of thinking beings, by offering your living bodies as a holy sacrifice, truly pleasing to God. Do not model yourselves on the behaviour of the world around you, but let your behaviour change, modelled by your new mind. This is the only way to discover the will of God and know what is good, what it is that God wants, what is the perfect thing to do" (Rm 12: 1-2). He emphasized to them that worship is not limited to formal rites, but is effective in the daily rituals of living with others. "Treat everyone with equal kindness; never be condescending but make real friends with the poor. Do not allow yourself to become self-satisfied. Never repay evil with evil but let everyone see that you are interested only in the highest ideals. Do all you can to live at peace with everyone" (Rm 12:

16-18). No area of endeavor should be outside this "offering . . . as a living sacrifice." The spontaneity and ordinariness of living worship is evident in Paul's encouragement to everyone to be concerned for the way work is done. "Work for the Lord with untiring effort and with great earnestness of spirit. . . .

If your gift is prophecy, then use it as your faith suggest; if administration, then use it for administration; if teaching, then use it for teaching. Let the preachers deliver sermons, the almsgivers give freely, the officials be diligent, and those who do works of mercy do them cheerfully" (Rm 12: 11; 6-8). For Paul, worship, a way of life which brings us and the whole world home to God, finds its symbolic shape in the Eucharist. Thus, Eucharist is seen as the center-piece, the most focused form, of the primary activity of the Church: the liturgy of life in each moment — the sacrifice of praise and thanksgiving.

Christians are a people who know the living God as present and active in their midst. They are familiar with the history of the relationship between God and his people, which shows God to be faithful and concerned. They know the Lord Jesus as a clear and challenging revelation of God and of what it means to live humanly. All this leads them to a deep sense of wonder and gratitude for all that is and has been, and a firm commitment to realize the possibilities that can be by allowing the divine love to be present in them. It is in their daily living that the people are eucharist for their

The Sacrament of Christian Life

world, proclaiming, revealing, and making present the God who is love.

In assuming their role as proclaimers of the good news, the Christian people relive the experience of the disciples on the road to Emmaus (Lk 24: 13-35). The two men were joined on the road by Jesus, whom they failed to recognize. The disciples were aware of the events of the passion of Jesus, and of the reports of his resurrection. But, again, they failed to see these within the context of the prophetic tradition and missed the meaning of all that had happened. Jesus proceeded to explain the Scriptures to them, beginning with Moses and the prophets and leading up to the experience of his life among them. Still, they did not grasp the full meaning of what was said until Jesus blessed and broke bread with them. "Their eyes were opened and they recognized him" (Lk 24: 31). They immediately returned to Jerusalem to share the good news.

The same pattern is apparent in the action of the Christian Eucharist. Jesus, who walks with us, is often unrecognized, even by those who are well acquainted with the story of God's people. In the liturgy of Eucharist, the Scriptures are read and interpreted, beginning with the prophets and continuing through the experience of Jesus of Nazareth. The Christian community recalls the meaning of the prophets and the whole tradition of the people of God. Yet, the recognition of the risen Jesus and the acceptance of him as Lord comes about most clearly in the "breaking of the bread." Communion with the Lord sends the people forth praising God and preaching the good news in all the moments of their lives.

A People Become Church

In the experience of the ritual action of Eucharist, the people become Christian community, become church, become the body of Christ. It is here that they are incorporated into the life and mission of Jesus; that they come to know the Father in coming to know the Son; that they gradually take on the mind of Jesus in seeking the meaning of life in this world. The ritual action of Eucharist is powerful when it is allowed to penetrate the life and action of the people, and transform them into an effective embodiment of the love that is God, a sacrament of his presence.

Yes, the ultimate action of Eucharist is the transformation of the people into the body of Christ. All of the symbolic action, including the consecration of the symbols of bread and wine, is focused on this result: that the people become the living presence of the risen Jesus both to God and the world. The result of the transformation of the bread and wine into the body of Jesus is not that Jesus may be adored, but that Jesus may be embodied in the people who can then be his presence in the world. In the early centuries of Christianity, the term ''body of Christ'' was most commonly applied to the community of believers. Later in history, it came to designate almost exclusively the consecrated species to be adored as the visible presence of Jesus who is Lord. The documents of Vatican II restore the identification of the

The Sacrament of Christian Life

assembled community as the body of Christ, "every liturgical celebration . . . is an action of Christ the Priest and of his Body, which is the Church" (SC 7). The documents describe the eucharistic action as a summit moment gathering in all the activity of the body and as a fount from which the power of love flows into the whole living experience (SC 10).

Assembly of the People

The first action in the ritual of Eucharist is the gathering of the people. From all kinds of family situations, from all types of work places, from the youngest to the oldest, from the richest to the poorest, from the powerful and from the oppressed, from the learned scholars and from the untutored illiterates — a people assembles in the name of Jesus. They come to praise God for his goodness; they come to plead with God for mercy and forgiveness; they come to find courage and strength in the fidelity of God; they come to share with Jesus the anguish of rejection or failure; they come seeking refuge from the chaos and violence in their lives; they come to be comforted in times of illness or abandonment. They come to pour into the sacramental action of Eucharist their diverse experiences of living and of the presence of God. This gathering of the people is the first step in the formation of the body, the church.

Rite of Reconciliation

As a people assembled in all their diversity, they seek to be made whole in the unity of divine love. The rite of reconciliation includes an acknowledgment of their weaknesses and their sins which threaten the well-being of the body. No body can function with its parts at odds with each other, with a lack of coordination, or with limitations placed on participation in the life of the whole. Individual Christians who do not surrender wholeheartedly to the life and mission of Jesus can impede the life and work of his body, the church. The healing love of God can bind them together in Christ into an effective community of faith. Recognition of their need, and acceptance of the healing activity of Jesus leads the gathered assembly a step closer to transformation into a community of love.

Liturgy of the Word

In the readings from the Scriptures, the life stories of their ancestors and of Jesus the Christ, the people are immersed in the faith tradition. They are put in touch with the God who is with them, the Savior who breathes his Spirit of life into them, and the centuries of life experience that have led the community of believers to an understanding of the activity of God in our midst. The Word of God is a human word which seeks to express the reality of the divine presence. It, too, is a sacrament — a vital symbol of the lived experience of a people through which they came to identify and know their God. In the ritual of the Eucharist, the Word of God symbolizes both the human words that are the Scriptures and the divine Word who is the Son. Both are revelations of the Father.

The Sacrament of Christian Life

The assembled people hear, in the readings from the Old Testament, the stories of a God who has shown himself to be one who is always with Israel, who is faithful even when deserted, who chooses the Israelites as his own people not because of their worthiness but because of his love, who relates with his people in mercy and compassion, who asks them to live in justice and peace with one another. At times, the Israelites distort or misunderstand this God, regarding him as a hard task-master, as one who punishes the wicked and destroys his enemies, as exclusively their God who favors them above all others. At times, they succumb to the lure of power or wealth and abandon Yahweh in favor of the popular idols of other nations, thus losing a sense of their own identity in the worship of false gods. The experience of the exile and the return to their own land form the people into the Jewish community as Jesus knew it. In the renewal of the covenant and the rebuilding of the Temple, the Israelites become a renewed people of God. Through all of these experiences, over the course of many centuries of living in a variety of historical and cultural circumstances, the people of Israel come to recognize and to know the God who is with them and for them always and everywhere.

Today, as a Christian community, assembled for liturgy, listens to the history out of which it comes, the God of Israel can be known and recognized in the midst of their own lives. A story of compassionate love in a far away country thousands of years ago can be strikingly similar to a recent happening within this community. The call of the prophets for the ancient Israelites to give up their idols and return to the ways of Yahweh can be a powerful challenge to contemporary society to replace the competition, the greed, the violence and the selfishness of today's world with the concern for others, the simplicity of lifestyle, the peace and gentleness which characterize the way of a loving God. The reality of life begins to come into focus in a way which gives meaning and possibility to seemingly useless situations.

The revelation in Jesus becomes clear in the readings from the New Testament. The early Christian communities were committed to a lifestyle that had been manifested in the experience of Jesus. His presence among them had transformed them into a people of peace and gentleness and concern for one another. They were enabled to live in joy amidst a hostile and challenging society, recognizing goodness and opposing the evils they could see. What stands out in the story of their life as a Christian community is their conviction of the presence of the risen Jesus in their midst, and their undying resolve to continue his mission in this world: to make the Father known to all. The struggles of the apostles and the early missionaries are only part of the story; the divisions and trials within the various communities reflect the reality of daily Christian living. The situation has not changed basically in the history of Christianity. Today's leaders and missionaries face hostility and threats, even to the giving of their lives for upholding gospel values in corrupt societies. At the same time, the Christian people are frequently at odds with one another over the ordinary daily living of gospel

The Sacrament of Christian Life

values within their own communities. Indeed, the writings of Paul and John and Peter can speak directly to a Christian community of our day in terms of their own experience.

Paul speaks so clearly of the demands placed on the lives of those who would be disciples of Jesus. "You must give up your old way of life. . . . Your mind must be renewed. . . . There must be no more lies: You must speak the truth to one another, since we are all parts of one another. Even if you are angry, you must not sin: never let the sun set on your anger. . . . Anyone who was a thief must stop stealing; he should try to find some useful manual work instead, and be able to do some good by helping others that are in need. Guard against foul talk; let your words be for the improvement of others, as occasion offers, and do good to your listeners. . . . Never have grudges against others, or lose your temper, or raise your voice to anybody, or call each other names, or allow any sort of spitefulness. Be friends with one another, and kind, forgiving each other as readily as God forgave you in Christ" (Ep 4: 22-32). These words of advice are just as relevant to the Christian community of today, and can be readily applied in the lives of the members.

John speaks in terms of love, a love that can be seen in deeds. "We can be sure that we are in God only when the one who claims to be living in him is living the same kind of life as Christ lived" (1 Jn 2: 5-6). "This is the message as you heard it from the beginning: that we are to love one another; not to be like Cain, who . . . cut his brother's throat . . . to hate your brother is to be a murderer. . . .

Mary Peter McGinty

This has taught us love — that he gave up his life for us; and we, too, ought to give up our lives for our brothers. If a man who was rich enough in this world's goods saw that one of his brothers was in need, but closed his heart to him, how could the love of God be living in him? My children, our love is not to be just words or mere talk, but something real and active" (1 Jn 3: 11-19). How eloquently these words resound in a world filled with violence and greed, with a crying need for love.

Peter extols the glory of faith in Jesus Christ, a faith that is "tested and proved like gold. . . . You did not see him, yet you love him; and still without seeing him, you believe; and you are sure of the end to which your faith looks forward" (1 Pt 1: 7-9). That faith is a call to a new life: "Free your minds, then, of encumbrances; control them, and put your trust in nothing but the grace that will be given you when Jesus Christ is revealed. Do not behave in the way that you liked to before you learnt the truth . . . be holy in all you do . . . let your love for each other be real and from the heart. . . . Be sure, then, you are never spiteful, or deceitful, or hypocritical, or envious and critical of each other. You are new born" (1 Pt 1: 13-15, 22; 2: 1-2). The way of faith leads into every aspect of life: "Always behave honourably among pagans so that they can see your good works for themselves. . . . Accept the authority of every social institution. . . . God wants you to be good citizens. . . . Have respect for everyone and love for our community" (1 Pt 2: 12-17). In sum, Peter calls for faith to be expressed in deeds:

The Sacrament of Christian Life

"You should all agree among yourselves and be sympathetic; love the brothers, have compassion and be self-effacing. Never pay back one wrong with another, or an angry word with another one; instead, pay back with a blessing. That is what you are called to do" (1 Pt 3: 8-9).

Perhaps the most powerful writings of all the Scriptures are the gospel accounts of the experience of Jesus. For here, we encounter the very Word of God in our own milieu — the living God who enters our world as one of us and shares our way of life. The Jesus who steps forth from the pages of the gospel accounts shows us in words and actions who God is and enables us to know him on our own terms. He loves the Samaritan woman not for who she is or what she has done; he loves her, and that fact transforms her life. He loves Zaccheus not because Zaccheus has earned his love or because he approves of his business deals; he loves him. He loves Magdalen not for her attractiveness or her way of life; he loves her. His healing love reaches out to the servant of a pagan centurion as readily as to the children of Israel. He challenges the Pharisees and reproaches the money-changers; he reproves the ambition of Peter and the sons of Zebedee; he withstands the threats and the violence of the chief priests and the Romans; while he loves them. Jesus may confront, but he does not reject: "whoever comes to me I shall not turn him away; because I have come from heaven, not to do my own will, but to do the will of the one who sent me" (Jn 6: 37-39). The revelation he embodies is the unconditional and faithful love of the Father which alone is

Mary Peter McGinty

capable of transforming this world and all of humanity into the harmony of creative life.

The life of Jesus shows us how this love can be humanly expressed and experienced. The greater part of his life was ordinary, lived in a small village of an obscure and oppressed nation. We frequently think of Jesus in terms of the major events reported in the gospels. In fact, he lived thirty years in obscurity, going about the very ordinary tasks of daily living. This is where (and how!) he "grew in wisdom and grace." This is where he came to the maturity of human skill and knowledge that marked him as a unique person. Mary and Joseph, the older people of the village, the children with whom Jesus played, were the ones who cultivated the human characteristics of his personality.

These characteristics appear in full bloom as Jesus takes up his active ministry. Following the ministry of John the Baptist in preparing the way of the Lord, Jesus accepts his confirmation in the Spirit: "This is my Son, the Beloved; my favour rests on him" (Mt 3: 17). Well versed in the traditions of his people, Jesus steps forward to present the good news of the kingdom through his own life and teaching.

When he meets the woman taken in adultery, or speaks the beatitudes to the assembled crowd, Jesus is bringing into focus the fruits of his learning throughout the years of his growth. Of the many lessons we can draw from his life, surely one of the most compelling is the importance of attentiveness to the ordinary events of each day. For, it is here we are shaped into the persons who can be sensitive to the needs

58

The Sacrament of Christian Life

which confront us at the most unexpected times and in unforeseeable ways. Indeed, the gospel readings can often catch us off guard and challenge us quite directly in terms of our own life experience.

The homily is meant to serve precisely this purpose, to relate the experience reflected in the Scripture readings to the events in the lives of the present congregation. Eucharist is meant to be a moment of worship, of meaning and challenge for the Christian community. Modern life moves at such a rapid pace that it is easy to lose sight of the significance of events, especially of those everyday happenings which we tend to think of as insignificant, which we do not identify with worship. As a community, gathered in the presence of the risen Jesus, the Christian people can touch once more the presence of divine action and the basic meaning of life in this world. They can face the challenge of living their particular situations as expressions of God's loving presence here and now. Steeped in the tradition of a people who are chosen and loved for no merit of their own, they can begin to realize the goodness of all that is and the strength of God's love to bring life out of impossibility. Captives can be freed, the hungry can be filled, the sick can be healed, violence can be tamed, greed can be converted to giving, power can be channeled to good, hearts can rejoice, and people can live together in peace. Not by magic, not by divine decree, not by the intervention of the gods, but by the persistent way of life of a community of faith. In the homily, the meaning and the challenge of living as Christians in this particular

59

setting — the liturgy of each moment — is clearly set before the assembly. For each one present, the word must take root and bear fruit. Thus, this people become the body of Jesus, his effective presence, making it possible for the love of the Father to touch and transform human living. The ordinary living of the men and women who know the risen Jesus becomes Christian sacrament in and for the world. This is the power of Eucharist.

Liturgy of the Eucharist

Following the homily, the assembled community turns its attention from the Word of Scripture to the Word made flesh. After proclaiming its Christian faith in the words of the Creed and making explicit its concerns for the world and the life of the community, the people enter into the ritual celebration of the paschal meal. The gifts of bread and wine are brought to the altar, uniting in symbol the lives of those who offer the gifts with the life of the risen Jesus who presides at this meal. The people express their willingness to offer the whole of their lives to continue the mission of Jesus in this world. They want to be one with him in pursuing the will of God for all. And so they unite with Jesus in his total gift of himself as life for others. God gave himself totally not only in becoming what we are, but in his humanity living totally for others and handing over his life for the salvation of all humanity. For a person to ask to be one with Jesus is to be prepared for a total commitment that reaches into every moment of the day. That commitment is at once Father-

The Sacrament of Christian Life

centered and other-centered. Jesus is always turned to the Father, in praise of his goodness and in gratitude for his mercy. At the same time, he is always sensitive to the needs of the people he encounters and the countless expressions of the Father's presence which fill each day. The Christian community that enters into personal union with the risen Jesus through the symbols of the bread and the wine assumes the way of life that is his: Father-centered in praise and gratitude, other-centered in care and vitality.

When the eucharistic action moves to the transformation of the symbols of bread and wine as the embodiment of Jesus, the Christian community is caught up in that transformation. The risen Jesus is present, can be known, is located in the eucharistic symbols of bread and wine; they are his body. A body that is broken, as the bread is broken; that is poured out, as the wine is poured; that is meant to be shared as a source of life, a sign of solidarity and unity. A body that embraces the centuries of tradition and history following upon the experience of exodus. A body that assumes the full meaning of a Word made flesh, of a covenant renewed in the living experience of the God-man, of a gift of self in death at the hands of merciless men, and of an entry into full human living at the hands of a lovingly creative Father.

Yet, these symbols of bread and wine transformed into the body of Jesus are not there to be looked at and admired. This is Jesus, a Jesus who is giving himself in this bread/wine body. He is asking to be received so that he can share his life, his mission. He is asking to enter into communion with

61

Mary Peter McGinty

those who accept his way of life, his message. He is asking to shape a community who will be identified as ''Jesus people,'' as Christians. The people assembled are the living symbol, the key symbol, the embodiment of the risen Lord. They are a people who offer themselves as a sacrifice of praise and thanksgiving — a eucharistic community. They are a people who are truly signs of loving care and service, who cannot be indifferent to and unconcerned about the events of the day, who avoid division and animosity in all its forms. They are a people who have accepted the loving self-gift of Jesus himself, a people constantly renewed in the action of Eucharist to confront the changing circumstances of each day. They are a people who share a vision of human life, who find meaning in the world and in human history through the celebration of Eucharist.

To accept communion with Jesus, to share the bread and the cup, is to enter into the full experience of human living and the challenge of resurrection. Christians who share the life of the risen Jesus in the eucharistic bread and wine are likewise transformed into his body. In the elements of bread and wine, broken, poured out, and shared, Jesus is personally present as a source of life and unity in this community which is now sacrament, body of Jesus. The eucharistic action which does not culminate in this transformation is short-circuited. For, the action of Eucharist is meant to be a ''missa,'' a sending forth to proclaim the good news to all the nations. The mission of Jesus is to make the Father known. On the human scene, this calls for human expression in the presence

The Sacrament of Christian Life

and activity of his body — the Christian community of those who share his life and his Spirit. This people is called forth and empowered in Eucharist. And this people is sent forth to live in the world. The eucharistic action gathers in all the fragments of living of this particular community and gives them meaning in the light of the experience of Jesus and the fidelity of God. And it challenges Christians to recognize the opportunities for transformation which are present in the most seemingly insignificant moments. Becoming the body of Jesus in the action of Eucharist is a reality, only when it reaches out into the living experience of the body. The love of the Father must touch a life and make a difference. Then, the presence of Jesus is felt. Then, the Eucharist is an effective action. To limit Eucharist to the ritual is to miss the point: to be the body by which Jesus can continue his mission in and for the world.

MATRIMONY

A sacrament which is basic to Christian living in ways very similar to Eucharist is the sacrament of Matrimony. Marriage becomes a Christian sacrament not only because it is celebrated in a ritual action of the Christian community, but because of the way it is lived in the ordinary circumstances of everyday events. The sacrament is, first of all, the committed *life*, and only secondarily the rite by which the life is entered. While Eucharist focuses our attention on the divine love expressed in the humanity of Jesus, and on the intensity of love which led Jesus to give of himself so completely on our behalf, Matrimony focuses our attention on human love and friendship as embodiments of divine love. The eucharistic community becomes body of Christ and lives out that sacramental identity in the events of every day. The family community, already the body of Christ through eucharistic commitment, highlights the fidelity, unity and self-giving of a love that incarnates the divine self-gift.

Married love reveals in human terms the character of divine love. Marriage is a covenant relationship, not entered into out of obligation, but freely in gracious self-giving. "My beloved is mine and I am his" (Sg 2: 16) echoes the promise of Yahweh in sealing the new covenant with the people of Israel: "I will be their God and they shall be my people" (Jr 31: 34). The relationship is the basis for the life, gives meaning and strength to every moment. The covenant is simple and complete: "I shall give you the gift of my love" (Sg 7: 13). There is no end to this relationship: "my love for you will never leave you and my covenant of peace with you will never be shaken" (Is 54: 10). Such is the love that binds two Christians in marriage.

The Experience of Love

Love is something we experience in relationships with others. To know what love is we need to be loved and we need to understand what is involved in the gift of self to another. We can begin to understand the love of God for us only when we sense some human expressions of fidelity and

64

The Sacrament of Christian Life

real indications of what love is: to be accepted as we are, to be respected in all our uniqueness, to be forgiven our faults and failings, to be supported and encouraged in our efforts, to be challenged and stimulated to reach our potential, to be invited to share a personal union, to live in communion with others. Without the human expression of these characteristics, we can never come to know the reality of love, to know who God is. And so, we are very important for each other, as sacraments of God's love, as revelations of the God who is love.

Marriage is a paradigm of human love and friendship, a prime example of mutual self-giving. It is a willingness to share life at the expense of self-interests, to place the well-being of another above one's own, to forge a union of mutual dependence while fostering the uniqueness of each person, to be a life-giving energy within the world. For Christians, all this is true within the specific perspective and vision of the mission of Jesus to bring all peoples to an awareness of God's love for us. Christian marriage involves a decision on the part of two people who have already committed themselves to be sacraments of God's love for others. It specifies that baptismal commitment to the Christian community in terms of one person, to enter into a personal relationship which mirrors that of God with humanity, and that of Jesus with the Christian community. As Vatican II says, "A love like that, bringing together the human and the divine, leads the partners to a free and mutual giving of self, experienced in tenderness and action, and permeates their whole

65

Mary Peter McGinty

lives . . . this love is actually developed and increased by the exercise of it'' (GS 49). Marriage involves a decision to be a revelation of God's love to another through a total gift of self and a genuine acceptance of the other, a gift that knows no limits and remains constant forever. It is a decision to enter into a personal communion which places no conditions on the circumstances within which the relationship evolves or on the consequences which may emerge. In the Christian context, this commitment is not only private and personal between two persons, it has meaning within and gives expression to the life-giving relationship of God with his people. The marriage union draws strength from and gives life to the eucharistic community as it lives out God's love-relation with the world as body of Christ. The public ritual of the marriage vows, celebrated within the liturgy of eucharist, calls attention to the mutual involvement of the community and the individual couple in this sacramental expression of divine love. The mutual commitment entered into at baptism is made more specific in the responsibilities of the marriage union. The individuals begin a new way of life within and on behalf of the community. To emphasize this point and to express it sacramentally, some Christian communities are encouraging couples to celebrate their union with the community at a Sunday liturgy. A more simple ceremony involves the whole assembly of believers in witness to and celebration of the covenant sealing. Such an occasion serves to recall to the community its commitment to be God's people and to live out the mission of Jesus. It emphasizes to the

The Sacrament of Christian Life

newly united couple their role within the body, and the full support that surrounds them in living out their relationship. Thus, covenant becomes more effective as it is seen and experienced in human lives.

The Gift of Self

Marriage is a sacramental action which is effective in all the moments of daily life, in the give-and-take of relationships. It has its own ritual expression in the act of marital intercourse with all its symbolism of gift of self for life, of surrender and acceptance, of communion in love. The gift of self symbolized in the giving of one's body in a love union echoes Jesus' eucharistic gift of himself as he offers his body for communion with a faith community. But this ritual action of physical intercourse is short-circuited if it does not lead to a day-by-day lived communion where that love is made evident in a relationship which pervades the ordinary events in life. The ritual act is meant to be both a summit which gathers up the love-living in each day, and the source of strength and creativity for each day to come. Each day should see a growth in respect, patience, awareness of and acceptance of difference, concern, willingness to give, real union of persons. Love is expressed and felt in very simple ways — washing the dishes, stopping to listen, noticing a change — and in trying circumstances — suffering through an illness, attempting to reconcile opposing views, dealing with the sometimes disruptive influence of other people. Such love, in its fidelity and integrity, is a powerful sign in the lives

67

Mary Peter McGinty

of the two persons, of the family, and of the broader community. It is truly a sacrament, an instrument for making God's presence known in a way which is actually transforming.

Without the effective sacramental action of marriage in its midst, the Christian community will find itself impoverished in seeking the meaning and challenge of life in this world. With it, the occasions for being touched by love are multiplied. Marriage initiates a new common existence for the two persons involved. They move out of individual lifestyles into a shared identity, calling for a great deal of cooperation and compromise. No longer do they function as "I" but gradually take on the identity of "we." For the Christian community, they become sacrament of personal union, shared living, fidelity, friendship, and of the possibility of real community in our fragmented society.

The life-giving power of love is striking in the conception and birth of a child. The marriage union again echoes the eucharistic union of Jesus and his disciples. As Jesus becomes one with the Christian community in the gift of his body, his Spirit of love is embodied and sent forth to speak that love to the world. So, too, in the marital act of physical union of bodies, love is embodied in a child who carries the integrity and fidelity of the parents' love into human life. The two are indeed one flesh in the infant they hold as a fruit of their love. All that they are for each other lives in this tiny body, dependent on them for life and yet wholly independent as a person to be uniquely cherished and nurtured. The

68

The Sacrament of Christian Life

life that comes from creative love is precious. It is sacrament, a sign of the love that conceived it, and an instrument that makes that love effective in the family, the Christian community, and the larger society in which it lives. What a difference a child makes!

Vatican II, in its teachings, restores a balance to the understanding of married love as "an eminently human love because it is an affection between two persons rooted in the will and it embraces the good of the whole person; it can enrich the sentiments of the spirit and their physical expression with a unique dignity and ennoble them as the special elements and signs of the friendship proper to marriage" (GS 49). The Council Fathers recognized in the marriage union an outstanding witness to faithfulness and harmony. While they continued to maintain the traditional teaching that "children are the supreme gift of marriage" (GS 50), they clearly stated that "marriage is not merely for the procreation of children. . . . Even in cases where . . . there are no children, marriage still retains its character of being a whole manner and communion of life and preserves its value and indissolubility" (GS 50).

Becoming a family is in many ways comparable to becoming church. Both family and church require a constant focusing on the root of life, the love of the living God, and a willingness to embody that love in the human way of life. The Christian family is within the community as a mini-church, a gathering of believers who accept Jesus as the very source of life and as the revelation of what it means to live in this

69

world. The family consists of persons who have committed themselves to live in union with one another, to give of themselves for the well-being of the other, to respect and honor the uniqueness of the other, and to work together as one body to make love effective in the lives they touch. The marriage commitment, as a specification of the eucharistic commitment, is all-encompassing, far-reaching, and never-ending. "Love is always patient and kind; it is never jealous; love is never boastful or conceited; it is never rude or selfish; it does not take offence, and is not resentful. Love takes no pleasure in other people's sins but delights in the truth; it is always ready to excuse, to trust, to hope, and to endure whatever comes. Love does not come to an end" (I Co 13: 4-8). To be the sacrament of God's love, the embodiment of his presence, is a full-time engagement.

A Recent Phenomenon

The ritual of marriage within the Christian community is a relatively recent phenomenon. Throughout the early centuries of Christianity, couples entered into marriage according to the customs of their particular culture and historical setting. The father of the bride's family held a prominent position in the rituals. Formal agreements were entered into in advance of the nuptials and the bride was ceremoniously escorted to the house of the bridegroom where her father gave her into the care of her husband. The family and the civil society were the guardians of the integrity of the marriage relationship. For Christians, this union had a special mean-

The Sacrament of Christian Life

ing in terms of their relationship with Jesus and with the Christian community. As early as the time of Paul, Christian marriage was seen as a symbol of the relationship of Christ with his church (Ep 5: 21-33). Christian couples understood their commitment to one another within their commitment to Jesus and to the church through baptism and eucharist. The Christian significance of this union was sometimes expressed in the blessing of the bishop during the wedding festivities. For Christians, the "church" aspect of marriage gradually increased in importance, leading to much discussion of the civil and ecclesial responsibilities in the social institution of marriage. The church was reluctant to become involved in the financial contracts and family customs, yet was concerned to preserve the integrity of a love union that expressed the union of Christ with his church.

Marriage was not firmly established as a Christian sacrament with its own legal form until the Council of Trent. The Council of Florence (1438-45) explicitly named marriage as a seventh sacrament, a sign of the union between Christ and his Church. The Council of Trent (1545-63) identified marriage as one of the seven sacraments of the New Law, instituted by Christ and conferring grace. Beyond this identification, Trent also established the legal form for a valid marriage between baptized persons, declaring that a valid marriage must be celebrated in the presence of a priest and two witnesses. While this did not deny the authority of the state in regulating the secular aspects of the marriage contract, it effectively removed Catholic marriage from the

Mary Peter McGinty

secular realm. It is interesting to note that the Christian churches influenced by the Reformation reverted to the undifferentiated situation, in which the sacramentality of marriage was left unexpressed. For Catholics, with the introduction of legal and juridical concepts, the church came to speak of marriage in terms of a contract which involved the approval of the church community. Legality was carried a step further in the declaration that any valid marriage between baptized persons was in fact a sacrament. This fusion of the legality and the sacramentality of the marriage commitment is an important element in the historical development of this Christian sacrament.

Valid and Indissoluble

From the early centuries of Christianity, controversy and confusion have surrounded the identification of this common human experience. A major question has been, ''What constitutes a marriage?'' Is it the consent of the persons involved that constitutes the union? By this mutual consent, a personal union and common life is established. Or is it the consummation of the union in the act of sexual intercourse? This act expresses and fosters the recognized goals of the union: fidelity in relationship, the gift of life in children, the symbolism of indissolubility rooted in the union of Christ and his church. In the juridical context which has prevailed since Trent, the answer has been that a valid marriage is established through mutual consent; the contract becomes indissoluble with its consummation through intercourse.

The Sacrament of Christian Life

Much of the history of this sacrament has focused on the ritual actions in terms of validity and indissolubility. Initially, the Christian community recognized the marriage commitment as a specific way of living out the baptismal commitment to reveal the love of God as faithful and life-giving. A basic human experience, marriage, took on a fuller meaning in light of the revelation in Jesus of the intimate relation of God with his people. "If anyone loves me he will keep my word, and my Father will love him, and we shall come to him and make our home with him (Jn 14: 23). The understanding of this human relationship faced serious questions as the act of sexual intercourse (the sacramental act of love) was looked upon by some as evil in itself and by others as only permissible for the procreation of children and as an outlet for the inordinate desires of sinful humanity. "It is better to be married than to be tortured" (I Co 7: 9). Only gradually did a positive view return to prominence: that the sexual act is good in itself as created by God, and that it is a sacramental expression of the fidelity and self-giving embodied in the marital union. Vatican II makes a clear statement: "Married love is uniquely expressed and perfected by the exercise of the acts proper to marriage. Hence the acts in marriage by which the intimate and chaste union of the spouses takes place are noble and honorable; the truly human performance of these acts fosters the self-giving they signify and enriches the spouses in joy and gratitude" (GS 49). The whole life experience of the couple gives credence and meaning to the self-giving act of physical union.

Mary Peter McGinty

The lived experience of the marriage union in its totality is sacrament, the expression of the faithful covenant of God with his people, the embodiment of the risen Jesus in union with the church. As a Christian symbol, as a revelation of the fidelity of divine love, marriage is indissoluble. Not because it is legally proclaimed to be so, but because the love that is professed is unconditional, unlimited and forever. In the words of Vatican II, "the man and woman . . . help and serve each other by their marriage partnership; they become conscious of their unity and experience it more deeply from day to day. The intimate union of marriage, as a mutual giving of two persons, and the good of the children demand total fidelity from the spouses and require an unbreakable unity between them" (GS 48).

A Christian Sacrament

Marriage is a human institution that has existed since the beginning of human society. "The intimate partnership of life and the love which constitutes the married state has been established by the creator . . . it is rooted in the contract of its partners, that is, in their irrevocable personal consent . . . receiving its stability, even in the eyes of society, from the human act by which the partners mutually surrender themselves to each other. . . . For God himself is the author of marriage" (GS 48). It becomes a Christian sacrament when it exists within the context of a Christian faith community. In the rite of matrimony, a believing people witness to and celebrate the union of a man and a woman in their midst as

74

The Sacrament of Christian Life

a specific way to live their commitment to Jesus and to be a living presence of divine love in human history. Throughout each day of their lives, a Christian husband and wife provide the faith community with a lived experience of steadfast love as it works its way through the events of daily life. The meaning of self-gift, of unconditional love, of fidelity, of intimate presence becomes clear in the life of a Christian couple, of a Christian family. It is a powerful sacrament which shows forth the concrete reality of living the baptismal/eucharistic commitment to be the incarnation of the risen Lord in this place and time.

The goodness of marriage is beyond dispute. It is rooted in the divine act of creation. The marriage union that is deeply rooted in God is a dynamic reality of unconditional giving and receiving. Union places demands and calls for deep renunciation of self. It is an ideal to be cherished, but is difficult to achieve in the concrete. This is especially so in a society that accepts pre-nuptial contracts, cohabitation, pre-marital sex, elective abortion, and no-fault divorce. It is equally difficult to achieve the ideal marriage in a society that uses marriage as a means of stabilizing business deals, or in a society that continues to regard a wife as the property of her husband and to recognize polygamy as a way of life, or among people who consider love to be a temporary and casual experience with no commitments attached.

Yet, Christian marriage pulls the whole context together and attempts to live out the ideal within the limitations of a particular time and place. The marriage union serves as a powerful sign to the faith community and, in turn, draws strength from the faith tradition. The ritual ceremony of matrimony initiates this union of husband and wife as a specific witness within the life of the community, establishing a relationship of mutual support between family and community. The sacrament is lived out in the day-by-day experiences of the couple and continues to be ritually celebrated and challenged in the eucharistic assemblies.

Secular Marriage

Such an understanding of Christian marriage raises questions as to the sacramentality of every valid marriage. Marriage as a human institution is a covenant of love and a powerful force within the society, capable of revealing the fidelity of God to his people. Christian marriage adds the dimension of the revelation in Jesus Christ of divine love and the context of a faith community as sacrament of the loving presence of the risen Lord. The question remains as to the sacramentality of the marriage of baptized persons who have no explicit faith and no ties to a Christian community. Can this union be a covenant of love? Yes, indeed. Is it a Christian sacrament? That seems doubtful in view of the fact that no Christian faith or identity is expressed. Can this union be a revelation of the goodness and the fidelity of the God who loves without condition or limit? Indeed, it would seem so. Is this union a revelation of the Christ who brought the reality of God's love into human history? Hardly, when the

The Sacrament of Christian Life

persons themselves do not know this Jesus and the God he reveals through his body, the church.

Are we at a point of distinguishing what was earlier fused — the legality and the sacramentality of marriage? It would seem that there is good reason to do so. A union of two persons can be a valid marriage when it involves mutual consent and complies with the laws and customs of the culture and the historical time. That union is a Christian sacrament when it is a commitment to a way of life within a community of believers. The distinction recognizes the fact that the Christian sacrament of matrimony is not identified solely by the consent of the persons involved, nor by the physical consummation of the union. Rather, the entire lived experience of the man and the woman who enter into the marriage union is Christian sacrament. That presumes and requires an explicit faith commitment (baptism) and a faith community (eucharist). Human marriage is good in itself, is valid when it conforms to the laws and customs of a culture, is to be treasured and supported within a society. Faith situates this human contract in the context of the divine covenant in Jesus and thus empowers it to be Christian sacrament.

The emphasis that the Church places on the indissolubility of the marriage commitment has led some people to suggest that young couples might first enter into a secular marriage, grow in a covenant relationship, and then identify their union as a Christian sacrament in the rite of matrimony. Implicit in this suggestion is the possibility of terminating the union and not proceeding to the sealing of the covenant in a Christian ritual. While seeming to present a practical solution in societies which find permanent commitment difficult, there is a problem with such an arrangement. It ignores the basic sacramentality of all marriage unions as rooted in the love of God for his people. It implies that only Christian marriages are revelatory and covenantal. Christians do not have exclusive claim to unconditional fidelity in relationships; God does. The union of two people in a marriage relationship is a personal fulfillment of the creation process: "This is why a man leaves his father and mother and joins himself to his wife, and they become one body" (Gn 2: 24). The Christian era did not confer sanctity and dignity and permanence on the marriage union; Jesus merely reinforced a reality of creation that holds true for all of humanity: "What God has united, man must not divide" (Mt 19: 6).

Yet, the practice of the Church has not ignored the stress that may enter into human situations. St. Paul cites the intolerable living conditions that might result from the marriage of a Christian with an unbeliever: "They may separate; in these circumstances, the brother or sister is not tied: God has called you to a life of peace" (1 Co 7: 15). The Eastern churches maintain a principle of *economia*, permitting remarriage after divorce in certain circumstances and with specific conditions. The contemporary Catholic Church seems to recognize the possibility of terminating a union which may have been entered into for reasons other than covenant love. In traditional teaching, a valid and consummated marriage

The Sacrament of Christian Life

between two baptized Christians could never be dissolved. While the Church does not grant divorces, it does declare some marriages to be annulled. Today, the reasons for annulment have been broadened to include deficiencies in understanding, in covenant love, in maturity, in communication, as well as certain social or psychological disorders. The marriage union is permanent, being rooted in the unconditional fidelity of divine love. Yet, the pastoral practice of the Church continues in the tradition of prudent discernment in concrete situations and genuine concern for the well-being of the individuals involved.

Many questions need to be asked and the Christian community needs to continue clarifying the sacramentality of marriage and the role of the rite of matrimony in its life. The marriage commitment can be a powerful act of worship on the part of the spouses and of the Christian community in response to the God who calls us to himself: "I will betroth you to myself for ever, betroth you with integrity and justice, with tenderness and love; I will betroth you to myself with faithfulness, and you will come to know Yahweh. . . . You are my people" (Ho 2: 21-22, 24).

SACRAMENTS OF HEALING

RECONCILIATION

IN BOTH the Church as Christian community and the family as a mini-Church, there is always a need for healing. Wherever people live together, the frictions and frustrations of human relationships are inevitable. Love in its ideal form is pure joy, the lure of risen life. But the way to that fulfillment is fraught with the limitations and sinfulness of our meager attempts to become what we can be. The love of God has called us, individually and as a people, to move towards a life of personal communion in peace, justice, and harmony. The call has gone out from the first moment of creation and throughout the history of Israel. Yahweh wants to walk with his people and share life with them. The covenant with Yahweh, made explicit in the relationships established with Noah, Abraham, and Moses, and renewed through the prophets and Jesus, calls for a mutual gift of self. God, on his part, offers his faithful presence: to Noah and the whole of creation, "I establish my Covenant with you" (Gn 9: 8); to Abraham and his descendants, "I will be your God" (Gn 17: 8); to Moses and the people of Israel, "I will adopt you as my own people, and I will be your God" (Ex 6: 7); through the prophet Jeremiah, "I will make a new covenant with the House of Israel. . . . Then

The Sacrament of Christian Life

I will be their God and they will be my people" (Jr 31: 31, 34); to the disciples of Jesus, "This cup is the new covenant in my blood" (Lk 22: 20). The other side of the covenant relationship calls for a comparable gift of self by living in peace and harmony with God and neighbor and world: for Noah, God had a warning, "I will demand an account of every man's life from his fellow men" (Gn 9: 5); for Abraham, the covenant again reached all parts of his life, "Bear yourself blameless in my presence" (Gn 17: 2); for the stubborn Israelites in the desert, Moses was told to spell out the meaning of fidelity to the covenant in detailed form, "Yahweh, a God of tenderness and compassion, slow to anger, rich in kindness and faithfulness . . . yet he lets nothing go unchecked" (Ex 34: 6-7); the new covenant foretold by Jeremiah is one of deepest love and respect, "Deep within them I will plant my Law, writing it on their hearts. . . . They will all know me" (Jr 31: 33-34); for the disciples of Jesus, the relationship is identified as one of intimate love, "If anyone loves me he will keep my word, and my Father will love him and we shall come to him and make our home with him" (Jn 14: 23). It becomes increasingly clear that love calls forth love, that fidelity requires fidelity, and that covenant touches every aspect of life. God has established a covenant with all of creation, most intimately with the human persons who are capable of achieving a union of peace and harmony and justice with God and neighbor and world. Love is a personal relationship that requires mutual participation to be effective. It is indeed striking and awesome that

81

our God has called us to live *with* him and work *with* him to establish a world that truly expresses his love.

Our best attempts to respond to that call are often thwarted by our limitations as creatures. We do not see clearly, we do not recognize opportunities, we do not have the strength or the courage to take up the challenges, we do not have the support necessary to pursue a way of life. Each of us is born into a situation that provides us with certain possibilities and leaves us ignorant of a vast universe of people who differ from us. The circumstances in which we live encourage certain values and ways of life which we take as normal. Amid all the variety in the human world, it can be very difficult to hear and to identify the call to covenant love. God is known by many names and, through diverse traditions, takes on many different characteristics. His relation with human beings may be thought of as amicable or hostile; human response may be loving or fearful. God may be considered as controlling human life, capriciously intervening as he wills; he may be thought of as completely uninterested in the daily pursuits of human endeavor; or God may be seen as the faithful co-creator with humanity of a universe of peace and justice. Our knowledge of God, that he exists and what he is like, depends very much on the situation in which we live. The same God offers his gift of self in covenant love to all; the human situation presents and interprets that offer to the people. A response to the offer is therefore influenced by the traditions and the human lives that speak God to us.

A further limitation in our response to God's call to love

The Sacrament of Christian Life

comes from the circumstances in which we live and grow. God's love calls for a way of life that reflects the love we are given. It asks us to see people as God sees them, to cherish and nurture the whole of creation as a work of love, to seek peace and union among all peoples. In concrete settings, such ultimate values are not always easy to identify. Some children are born into desperate living conditions, where stealing is a means of survival and dominance of other persons is crucial to self-worth. The sharing, giving, and surrender which characterize love are totally foreign values. Others live in an atmosphere where possessions are the measure of self-worth, where superiority to others is all-important. There is no thought of having less so others can have more, nor of helping another to succeed. Customs and lifestyles differ greatly across the face of the earth, an earth which is called through Noah to be a universe of peace and justice, to be the realm of God. The particular society into which we are born and in which we are formed is not of our own making, but has been handed down to us through human and religious traditions. Yet, it is an essential element in our ability to know God and to hear his call to covenant love.

Finally, all of us bear personal responsibility one to another in the shaping of societies, in the handing on of the traditions. While we do not bear direct responsibility for what we have received, we are responsible for what we do and what we pass on to others. It is an astounding characteristic of the human person that limitations can be overcome, that lives can be improved, that conversions can take place. For,

83

Mary Peter McGinty

human beings are endowed with freedom to live decisively, and with a creative relation with the God who is love and whose active presence is assured. While we cannot discount the strong influence of history and of present experience, we cannot leave aside the strength of the human spirit and the alluring power of love.

Communities, whether they be religions, nations, business corporations, educational institutions, or families, bear a large part of the responsibility for the development of societies. The values they proclaim and the way they live out those values in daily life provide the basis for relationships within that situation. Will people admire superiority, exclusiveness, greed, domination, and egoism as the means to success? Or will they begin to notice the consequences of such attitudes on the lives of other people and turn instead to sensitivity, responsibility, genuine concern, sharing, other-centeredness as the way to establish a world of harmony and real progress? Lives can be seriously impaired and even destroyed through lack of sensitivity and attention.

Families are the most important factor in providing positive circumstances for the growth of the children and all the family members. Children are introduced to the values which will form them as persons in the family setting. What they see and hear from their earliest days emphasize for them those things which are important. Are people more valuable than things? Is it acceptable to exploit and abuse other persons, to take things from others and to damage whatever you touch? What happens to the people and things in the home has a

The Sacrament of Christian Life

lasting effect on a young family member. A life can be distorted, stifled, and permanently maimed in the wrong setting. On the contrary, where home is a place of love, life flourishes. A mother and father who love one another, cherish their children, protect and provide for the needy, and are genuinely concerned for the good of all are drawing forth the love of God which lies deep within the hearts of their children. They are indeed a mini-church, worshipping God in word and in deed, contributing to the formation of a society that can truly foster life. The world is not an easy place in which to live, providing much experience of suffering and futility for a human race that is so diverse and so finite.

The Reality of Sin

Yet, there is an even more serious element in our history as a human race and in our struggle to live humanly. That is the phenomenon we call sin. For sin adds a distinctive dimension to our failings — sin is deliberate, the product of human decision. Sin is so insidious precisely because it attacks the very source of life; sin is basically a rejection of love and a refusal to love. It prevents people from directing their lives in response to God's call towards the fulfillment of communion. Rather, sin positively causes a drastic alienation of the person from self, society and world with a vast array of consequences. It underlies the chaos we experience in our world: hatred, vengeance, destruction, wars. From the time of Cain and Abel, persons have hated those they considered to be favored over them or to have more of the

Mary Peter McGinty

world's goods than they deserved. Human history is filled with the stories of those who took revenge on people they considered to have wronged them in one way or another. Guilt is often to be placed on both sides in such cases: the favored one may indeed have used illegal or immoral means to achieve his status; the wrong which is avenged may indeed be a sinful exploitation or abuse of the avenger. Yet, the deliberate decision to hate or to harm is destruction of both persons, and seriously impairs the possibility for peace and justice. It is a direct rejection of love, since love places no conditions and withholds its gift from no one. When love is destroyed by greed and a desire to dominate, the consequences are disastrous. The world is not, and has never been, free from the devastation wrought by countless wars among nations who raise the sinful actions of individuals to the dimension of world conflict. The suffering and futility which result from the limitations of the human condition are raised to intolerable heights by sin.

Sin is an obstacle to full human living. On the personal level, sin alienates persons from themselves as they refuse to go out to others in genuine human concern, as they choose comfort and safety at the expense of freedom and responsibility. It is always a deviation, a turning away from what they can be, by their own deliberate choice. When young people choose to think of money as more important than knowledge, they will drop out of school to deal drugs on the street. Not only are they curtailing their own possibilities

86

The Sacrament of Christian Life

for development as human beings, but they are directly involved in destroying other lives through all the crimes of violence, abuse, exploitation, murder that are part of the drug scene. Or, when power over others is all-important, people will take any means to advance in the company they work for, ignoring the destruction of lives and families caused by their ruthless climb to the top. At the top, the same attitude will lead to corporate decisions which produce a big profit while cutting off the means of livelihood for countless numbers of employees. A nation with millions of unemployed persons has corporate executives who are worth billions of dollars! Persons with full potential to be loving and lovable human beings can become destructive forces, not only of themselves, but of countless others and of society as a whole.

Persons need to be turned around, redirected, healed. On a social level, sin is experienced as persons refuse to others the honesty, the respect, the concern they have a right to expect. It causes all the antagonisms that separate people, the prejudices, the stereotypes. It brings us so far from the simple command of the gospel: "Love one another; just as I have loved you, you also must love one another" (Jn 13: 34). Peoples of the earth are meant to live in harmony, not eliminating all differences, but blending the variety into a unity. The creative love of God makes it possible, but can only invite, not force, our participation. Sin can arise, in individuals or communities or nations, from a fear of rejection, a clinging to old hostilities, a desire for popularity. It can show itself in the many forms of indecision, apathy, disorder, injustice, exploitation. But, at the heart of sin is infidelity, the denial of love.

Healing Forgiveness

To accept love, to speak of conversion, to seek forgiveness, is to turn to God. There is no question of God's part: He loves, He is always forgiving, He accepts us as we are, He is for us. The question is whether we can accept His love. That involves the admission of a need to be re-directed in our lives. It involves a process of healing in order to live more genuinely. In the Christian community, Jesus Christ presents both the revelation of God's love and the experience of a lived human response. God's love for us is so intense that he "sent into the world his only Son so that we could have life through him" (1 Jn 4: 9). Jesus showed the quality of the divine love as he dealt with a variety of human situations: he talked with sinners and outcasts; he ate in the homes of tax collectors and the wealthy; he did not condemn public sinners, but called them to conversion; he led the proud and the powerful to new life. He showed the unconditional love that can be powerfully alluring, opening up new possibilities for human community. He also demonstrated the possibility for human participation in that expression of love through his own life experiences. All his life was God-oriented, with explicit admission of his dependence on the Father for all that he said and did. His whole life activity was geared toward

The Sacrament of Christian Life

leading people to know the Father. Such a mission led him to be totally other-oriented, with sensitivity to the needs of those he encountered and a sense of responsibility for the people at large. He sought not only to relieve the suffering of the neglected and the sick; he also tried to reach the hearts of the wealthy and powerful who could bring about more lasting changes in society. In his own life, Jesus experienced happiness and satisfaction, as well as rejection and hostility. Yet, he walked always in the presence of the Father's love and demonstrated the human ability to live in love. He realized to the fullest extent the meaning of covenant love and the necessity of love for healing and communion.

For Christians, liturgy plays an important role in this process of healing. The liturgies of baptism and eucharist have a long tradition of dealing with the need for forgiveness of sin and redirection of life. The sacrament of reconciliation addresses directly the communal need to become one people. As human persons, we need to be immersed in a context of faith, a living presence of God. In other words, we need sacramental actions; we need church.

The Christian context provides us with a number of opportunities to experience, to renew, to deepen our conversion, our turning to God, our forgiveness, our healing. The first and most radical experience is that of baptism which is meant to signify the basic commitment to a way of life, to come to know and follow Jesus, renouncing any previous goals in favor of a communal pursuit of the kingdom. This

Mary Peter McGinty

conversion has always been understood to include "forgiveness of sins." The role of baptism in the Christian life process will be addressed in a later chapter.

What has also been recognized throughout the lived history of Christianity but is not as clearly understood by many, is the role of Eucharist in forgiveness of sins. The Council of Trent speaks of the Eucharist as a medicine which frees us from daily faults and preserves us from serious sin. Every celebration of Eucharist begins with a rite of reconciliation in which the assembled community asks for the healing touch of God's love to unite them as one people in Jesus. Throughout the liturgy, the people give thanks for the love that sustains them and for the life of Jesus who has raised humanity from a sinful life and opened to all the way to a fullness of life. The liturgy of Eucharist is the primary sacrament of forgiveness, the ordinary reconciling of those who are striving to build the kingdom. As we have seen in the previous chapter, the eucharistic community gathers to celebrate the love of God expressed in the happenings of daily life. This is where the community senses the love of God in the risen Jesus and in the members of his body. Here is healing and strength in the process of becoming the kingdom.

Rite of Reconciliation

The new rite of reconciliation, mandated by Vatican II, is set within the context of this process of conversion. It is meant to be first of all what every liturgy is: a celebration of God's love as it is experienced in the lives of his people.

The Sacrament of Christian Life

Recognizing the Eucharist as the normal and ordinary sacrament of forgiveness, the liturgy of reconciliation celebrates a peak experience of many reconciling moments, externalizing the experience of forgiveness which has its meaning in all-the-time living. It proclaims a process that is going on. It is meant to be the fruit of a special experience: an Advent anticipation of the embodiment of God in Jesus of Nazareth; a Lenten recognition of the depth of commitment involved in becoming a Christian, and of the intensity of life inherent in resurrection. At times, a community or a group may undergo a traumatic experience brought on by illness, by crime, by war, by racial or ethnic division. The community needs to reconcile and become whole once more, to begin once more to live as one body. The sacrament of reconciliation then expresses and brings about some sense of a new beginning. The signs of the sacramental action affirm a deeper interior process: the laying on of hands testifies to the healing and reconciling that have taken place; absolution seals the acceptance of love. The priest, in the name of the community, pronounces the fact of forgiveness and loving acceptance. To receive the assurance that God and the community love us as we are bears with it a responsibility. We must love in like manner, forgiving others and doing all we can to promote God's peace and justice in the world we touch. Rejoicing and resolve accompany a creative acceptance of the love of God within the context of a responsible community, who experience a sense of walking in newness of life with a deepened realization that God loves them and forgives them. It is a moment of celebration and of challenge.

Healing is a simple, albeit difficult, process: accepting love and forgiveness into our lives. Ritual action provides the opportunity to experience that forgiveness and acceptance in human words and actions. The liturgy of reconciliation expresses the responsibility of the members of the community to and for each other, and the commitment to be one body, whole and vital, as a presence of the Lord. The people accept the love of God as a dynamic force in their lives which seeks to reach out to all the world. It is a moment of rejoicing and of resolve.

Development of the Rite

The sacramental experience of forgiveness within the Christian community has taken on a number of external forms. Never was there a doubt of the need for healing in the lives of the believers. Nor was there doubt that this was the work of the whole body. In the earliest initiation rites, following Jesus meant leaving behind a familiar way of life and entering into the Christian lifestyle. It meant a *metanoia,* a redirection of a life in terms of the covenant with the risen Lord, a death to any self-directed interests and a commitment to live a God-centered and other-centered vision. Becoming a Christian was indeed a new birth, a new beginning, with the past forgiven and the future open. It was a time to focus on possibility and opportunity, to respond to the initiative of God which offered the fullness of life in love. The ceremonies

The Sacrament of Christian Life

of baptism provided the initial communal experience of acceptance, of forgiveness, of belonging.

Through the centuries, the community has realized that the assembly for Eucharist requires that the body be healed of division and discord. God is not half-hearted in his relationship with his people. Nor can his people be partially committed in their relationship with him. This means that they need to be in communion with one another, reaching out in love to heal the hostilities and differences that may have grown among them. "Be friends with one another, and kind, forgiving each other as readily as God forgave you in Christ" (Ep 4: 12). The ritual of Eucharist begins with a reconciliation of those assembled, reflecting in ceremony the healing that has taken place. This is the ordinary way in which the Christian people confront their sinfulness toward one another in daily living, and allow the transforming love of God to draw them together as one people.

As the community developed, it became apparent that there were some in their midst who fell outside of this ordinary action. At times, a member might completely renounce the Christian belief and life; another might succumb to the self-gratifications that run counter to a Christian lifestyle. In so doing, these members had placed themselves outside the life of the community and publicly proclaimed their division from the body. In many cases, the community formally acknowledged this situation in what was termed "excommunication." When an individual sought to be returned to full status within the body, a ritual of penance came into practice. Since the break had been public, the healing process was also public. The whole community participated in the ceremonies of repentance, true metanoia, and loving forgiveness, climaxing in the restoration of the sinner to the full life of the worshipping community in Eucharist. Such occasions were undoubtedly effective experiences of the fidelity of God's love and the need for the support of a believing community to embody that love.

With the growth of monasticism and its accent on self-discipline and on the spiritual direction of the individual, with more focus on the individual and personal infidelities in Christian living, new forms of penance came into practice. Gradually, there developed an examination of the individual life and a concentration on the number and kinds of sins committed.

Retribution for wrongs done became a prime consideration, with specific acts of penance and certain prayers offered in payment for debts incurred by sin. The entire process moved into a juridical mode, with a priest assigned and empowered to pass judgment and impose sentence on the guilty individual. The community had less and less to do with a process which became ever more private, personal, and anonymous. The forgiveness was seen to come from God through the church to the individual. Unfortunately, it might have little, if anything, to do with the healing of the body so cruelly disturbed by sin. The call to be a people who show forth the love of God in their fidelity and love for one another was pretty well obscured.

The Sacrament of Christian Life

In Vatican II, the call to covenant love went forth again. The church is called to be a sacrament of God's love. All people are called to live in union with one another as a sign and an instrument of their union in God. "You must live your whole life according to the Christ you have received — Jesus the Lord; you must be rooted in him and built on him and held firm by the faith you have been taught, and full of thanksgiving" (Col 2: 6-7). The sacrament of reconciliation is to be just that: an experience of healing in the lives of the Christian people. Together, they recognize and acknowledge their difficulties in living as God's people; they observe and identify the causes of their infidelity; they recall and celebrate the marvels of God's love and the certainty of his presence in their midst; they confront the present and face the future with hope and assurance rooted in the love of God and in the experience of a supporting community of faith. "You are God's chosen race, his saints; he loves you, and you should be clothed in sincere compassion, in kindness and humility, gentleness and patience. Bear with one another; forgive each other as soon as a quarrel begins. The Lord has forgiven you; now you must do the same" (Col 3: 12-13). Once more the accent is on the body and on the daily living of all the members. What happens in ritual is a peak experience of faith and love which gathers in what has been done and which makes possible all that this people can do. It is not a moment of forgiveness, but a moment of celebration for the reconciling that has taken place and for the new life that is opened up. It is a realization in the concrete of the belief that God is available to us in the people among whom we live, especially in those who commit themselves to embody his love in human life.

Systemic Evil

In a relationship with a God who is love, it would seem that the life of God's people would be filled with happiness, security, and joy. And so it is meant to be. "I have come so that they may have life and have it to the full" (Jn 10: 10). The happiness of union, the security of being loved, the joy of loving and serving others — this is the life to which God invites his people. "As long as we love one another, God will live in us and his love will be complete in us" (1Jn 4: 12). Yet, the experience of many people is far different from this ideal. In some instances, it is possible to approach happiness in a family/community setting where the limitations are accepted, the inevitable hurts in living are healed, and the growth of each member is nourished. But for too many people, daily life is a continuing experience of rejection, oppression, manipulation, abuse, hostility, violence, exploitation — the exact opposite of love and the full reality of sin. Much of this experience of sin has been institutionalized, has become a way of life within societies and cultures. It is difficult enough to deal with the sins of individuals and the consequences they may have on families and communities. How much more difficult it is to deal with the kinds of systemic evil which afflict massive numbers of people who are powerless to rise above their situation or to work to alleviate

The Sacrament of Christian Life

the suffering it causes. In our renewed sense of interdependence as people of God, we are again realizing the obligation of all people to seek the transformation of the human society into a world where every one can live in peace and dignity. Here is the place for the sacrament of God's love, the Christian community of believers, to be that sign and instrument of union it is called to be, it has committed itself to be, in and for the world.

Sin has frequently been understood as the action of an individual in transgression of a law. The seriousness of the sin and the penalty for it were determined within a juridical system. What is becoming clearer in the vision opened up by Vatican II is that sin is predominantly to be seen in terms of what it does to persons. It is not only the sinner who suffers the consequences. As a rejection of love, sin has serious consequences for the self-image of a person whose offer of friendship is rebuffed. As a refusal to love, sin limits concretely the possibilities for growth and life that could have opened up for another. Life truly revolves around the experience of love; sin tampers with the very roots of personal identity and value. What sin does to the sinner is even more destructive. To reject love and to refuse to love results in an isolation that increasingly dries up the possibilities for life and growth. Turning away from others, becoming self-centered is a consequence of sin that can eventually destroy a person, leaving in place either an indifferent and apathetic human being or a vicious and hard-hearted being who cannot be recognized as human.

Mary Peter McGinty

Sin can be called an offense against God in the sense that it destroys what God has created. It is not that this action is evil because it transgresses the law of God. It is evil because it thwarts the creative process by which the world and all of humanity move toward the fullness of life. Sin diminishes life and puts obstacles in the path of development. It undermines the relationships of persons with each other, divides communities and the world society, and interrupts the natural evolution of the universe. Sometimes it is malicious and fully intended; sometimes it is the unconcern, the apathy, or the self-centeredness that refuses to care what happens to others.

The Healing Power of Love

The Christian community needs to exist within the world as a place where love is experienced as unconditional acceptance, where the vision of life is God-centered and other-centered, where human dignity is respected, where everyone cares and everyone matters. This body of Christ must be present as a counter force, a love force, to the violence and greed of sinful powers. For an individual to turn the world around is a rare phenomenon. Jesus changed the meaning of and the possibilities for human living by his life among us. He has opened the way to full risen life for all of humanity. The world continues to feel the presence of his revelation and of his lived values. Yet, the love of God is subject to rejection and cannot force the covenant union so ardently desired. The people of God, a communion of believers, an embodi-

The Sacrament of Christian Life

ment of God's love in Christ, should be able to make a difference in the society it is helping to form. Through his people, reconciled through Christ, God seeks to love the sinners, the needy, and the powerful, and thus to move the world a little closer to its goal, a communion of peace and justice.

ANOINTING

The life of the Christian community, the wholeness of the body, is disrupted by forces other than the limitations and sinfulness of its members. Individuals within the body are frequently confronted with the kinds of physical incapacities that radically alter their capabilities to function as productive members. Scientific advances in modern society have done much to identify and to alleviate many causes of human suffering. Some diseases have been literally wiped from the face of the earth through preventive measures such as vaccines. Defective functions of the body's resources are being labelled as genetic disorders; new ways of dealing with such defects are being discovered daily. Thousands of specialists and researchers devote their lives to searching out ways to help those who suffer debilitating physical ailments. They are committed to assuring for the disabled the best possible opportunity to live a full human life. The results are astounding! Added to this are the specialists and therapists and researchers who work tirelessly to restore normal activity to those who have been severely injured through accident, abuse, or congenital deformities. More and more "hopeless cases" are taking their place in the mainstream of society, in classrooms and in businesses in a wide variety of productive careers.

Yet, the restoration to fuller living does not reach everyone who suffers. Individual opportunities are limited by factors of time and finances and human concern. For some, the scientific advances do not come quickly enough to reverse an illness. Some are, or think they are, totally unable to enter into the system because of financial status. For some, there is no one to notice their need and begin to put them in touch with the opportunities which exist. Still others have no will to live and remain mired in a sea of depression, of self-pity. Some have just given up and accept their situation without hope of change. In all cases, the loving concern of others is crucial to a positive living situation and to the possibility for healing.

This is a significant point for a Christian community to ponder. For, society is becoming more and more intolerant of weak and unproductive members. The excitement of discovery wears thin in the long and excruciating period of implementation. The generous support elicited by a startling rehabilitation of a young life tends to diminish as the day-to-day treatments stretch into years of tedious work. The office worker in a wheel chair delays the elevator and gets in the way in a restaurant. A child who needs special help in school takes away funds that might be used for a music teacher for all the students. Old people and sick people are a drain on the economy and raise the cost of health insurance for

100

The Sacrament of Christian Life

the rest of society. Most of all, people feel uncomfortable in the presence of the ill or the handicapped and tend to avoid being with them. Yet, the weak and the unproductive members of society need to know from others that they are valuable and cherished members of society. They need to experience that unconditional love that accepts them as they are, values them as co-workers in the creative process of human life, and reaches out to help them in their need.

Illnesses and disabilities deeply affect the family and friends of the sufferer, and the society with whom they relate. To an individual, and often to a society with its intolerance of weakness, the onset of a chronic or terminal illness can be unbearable. To be anything less than healthy and fully alive appears unacceptable. For the individual, dependence on others and loss of control over one's own life are sufficient cause for despair. For the society, the cost of caring for an incapacitated person is economically and personally too demanding. Parents of newborn infants who are seriously handicapped are choosing to give the child for adoption rather than face a prolonged period of intensive care, depriving themselves and their families of pleasurable time and financial security. States are considering laws which limit access to medical resources for those who are less likely to recover fully; laws which allow a physician to assist a sick person to die, that is, to help someone commit suicide. Illness, suffering, dependence, weakness, limitation of control, lack of usefulness are feared with increasing intensity by people in today's society. On the other side are the resentment and the

Mary Peter McGinty

anger on the part of those who find another's illness intruding on their time and energy and finances, often drastically changing their whole way of life.

Care For One Another

Yes, there is a call for another kind of healing within the Christian community. There is a call to be a people who care for each other without placing conditions on that care; a people who express the compassion of Jesus in their sensitivity to the needs of others: "'Sir,' he said 'if you want to, you can cure me.' Jesus stretched out his hand, touched him and said. 'Of course I want to! Be cured!' And the leprosy left him at once" (Lk 5: 12-14); a people who love the most helpless and the most powerless and raise them up through their ministry of love. Today's individuals are crying out for the healing love of the Jesus who gave sight to the blind: "He laid his hands on the man's eyes again and he saw clearly; he was cured, and he could see everything plainly and distinctly" (Mk 8: 25). Jesus made the lame to walk: "The crowds were astonished to see the dumb speaking, the cripples whole again, the lame walking and the blind with their sight" (Mt 15: 31). Jesus raised the dead to life: "He cried in a loud voice, 'Lazarus, here! Come out!' The dead man came out, his feet and hands bound" (Jn 11: 44). Today's society can be healed by the love of the Jesus who took pity on the grieving widow and restored her only son to life: "He went up and put his hand on the bier and the bearers stood still, and he said, 'Young man, I tell you to get up'. And

102

The Sacrament of Christian Life

the dead man sat up and began to talk, and Jesus gave him to his mother'' (Lk 7: 14-16). Jesus grieved with the father whose young daughter had died, and restored her to her family: "Taking her by the hand he called to her, 'Child, get up'. And her spirit returned and she got up at once'' (Lk 8: 55-56). In each case, Jesus touches and speaks to the person, not avoiding but entering into the situation of suffering. In our world, this love of Jesus needs human expression, made possible by the existence of his body, the church. The Christian people are called to be sacrament, effective presence, of the compassion of Christ for the suffering persons of our time. They can touch lives in ways that are empowering and enabling, in the name of Jesus Christ.

Suffering, pain, and limitation are devastating experiences for human persons, whether they come upon us without warning or whether we have been awaiting them as inevitable expressions of human frailty. A young person is diagnosed as being terminally ill with leukemia. Suddenly, the priorities and the perspectives of the family shift dramatically. Attention turns to this individual member and the other family members experience a whole gamut of emotions. Coping with the normal routine of everyday becomes a struggle that seems unbearable. Perhaps the parents are unable to accept the fact and continue to seek further medical opinions and look for signs that the child is really quite normal. Their turmoil puts great strain on their relationship and takes its toll on the other children in the family. The sick child resents the limitations on his activity; the healthy children resent the attention given to and the demands made by their sick brother. The parents have to make adjustments in their work schedules, perhaps jeopardizing their jobs. They need to make increasing demands on friends and family to help in the ordinary chores of living. Life has become a struggle with which they are less and less able to cope.

Or consider the experience of a couple who find themselves confronted with the reality of aging. They knew it was coming; now it is here. No longer able to be employed full-time, they need to adjust to a constant togetherness that tests their patience and tolerance. Weakness and chronic pain are a cause of frustration and annoyance, limiting their ability to do the things they would like to do. The romantic vision of retirement years has given way to the stark reality of decreasing bodily integrity. They find themselves withdrawing reluctantly from activities and responsibilities that formerly filled their lives with usefulness. They necessarily depend on others to take care of a growing number of daily chores. It is easy to slip into an apathy and an indifference brought on by a sense of being powerless and useless.

Altered Life-styles

Illness or aging can alter an individual's style of life and capacity for involvement. And the incapacitated person inevitably affects the life of the family and the surrounding community. For the Christian, this calls for an honest evaluation of possibilities and a realistic adjustment of the responsibilities as a member of the body of Christ. At baptism, the

The Sacrament of Christian Life

individual and the community enter into a relationship which calls for acceptance and cooperation on both sides. The aim is to be a significant presence of the risen Jesus and to carry out his mission on behalf of the world. The community commits itself to support and nourish the individual; the individuals commit themselves to participate in the effective living of the body. At times, this relationship needs to be reconsidered in the light of new circumstances. An individual's way of cooperating in the mission of the body may be significantly altered by illness, handicaps, or aging. Those who were formerly pillars of strength, reaching out to alleviate the needs of others, now find themselves in need of assistance for their most basic needs. The family of the stricken child find themselves unable to reach out to others in the ways they did, unable to assume their normal responsibilities within the community. Instead, they rely on members of the community to assist them in doing the most ordinary things, cooking meals or walking the dog.

The community needs to come forward in a renewed relationship with the individual that not only addresses the concerns of its newly weakened member, but identifies the ways in which that member can continue to be a strong participant in the life of the body. A person who lives calmly in the midst of suffering, an ill child who reflects a serenity and a loving concern for others in spite of severe limitations, are in their lives powerful revelations of divine love for the whole community. A couple who stand as an example of fidelity and unconditional love in the midst of increasing incapacities are a most effective experience of the presence of the risen Lord for the community that shares their life. Support and acceptance on the part of the family and the community give meaning to a life that is not diminished or abandoned but continues to enrich the whole community in its diverse expression of God's presence in this world.

A Community Ritual

From the beginning of Christianity, the community has cared for the sick and the weak in its midst. Prayer on behalf of the community and ritual anointing with oil were the common expressions of this concern. "If one of you is ill, he should send for the elders of the church, and they must anoint him with oil in the name of the Lord and pray over him. The prayer of faith will save the sick man and the Lord will raise him up again; and if he has committed any sins, he will be forgiven" (Jm: 14-16). At first, it was the elders of the community who carried out these ritual actions in the name of the whole body. They brought oil consecrated by the bishop to the bedside of the sick and anointed the individual as a sign of God's promise of life and the community's commitment of support. Historically, the rite of anointing came to be associated more and more with the moment of death. Penance became a major focus in the preparation for entrance into risen life and, consequently, the rite was delegated exclusively to a priest. The anointing became one of the rituals identified as the "last rites." Penance, anointing, and viaticum were seen as the Christian preparation for death.

The Sacrament of Christian Life

In practice, the anointing became the "extreme unction" reserved for the dying, and even administered to those already dead. For Christians, the appearance of a priest at a sickbed to anoint the sick person was a sign of the end. The ritual went from an expression of God's love and the community's concern to a guarantee of safe passage across the boundary of death. From a support to enable the person to live well in changed circumstances, it became a support to die well. In fact, the rite of extreme unction developed into a highly individualistic ceremony outside the experience of many of the Christian people. And it lost most of its significance for supporting the person in his/her attempts to live through the events of daily life.

Renewed Meaning

Vatican II radically changed the practice of this ancient ritual. This is noted in the restoration of the term used to identify the rite: from extreme unction it has become the sacrament of anointing of the sick. The emphasis is again placed on the activity of the members of the community in caring for and supporting those who are ill or weak, in assisting them to find meaningful ways of fulfilling their commitment to carry out the mission of Jesus in this world. The ritual, as far as possible, is to be a communal action with the presence of the worshipping community as an effective sign of the presence of divine love. As such, it conveys a strong message to the members of the body as well as to the individual sick person. The eucharistic community, which

107

constantly renews its commitment to be a presence of love, brings that commitment to bear in the particular situations of illness and aging that confront it in the individual members identified in the rite of anointing.

The life of the community depends on these sacramental moments which focus attention on the various dimensions of need on the process of daily living. Those who are well may benefit greatly from this contact with sickness or aging, with the witness of often heroic living in spite of increasing limitations. The Christian life is a communal affair, the life of a people. One effect of sacramental rituals is to focus attention on the wide variety of experience encompassed in that life.

The sacrament of anointing is to be distinguished from penance and from viaticum. Illness is not to be connected with guilt or sin: "'Rabbi, who sinned, this man or his parents, for him to have been born blind?' 'Neither he nor his parents sinned,' Jesus answered " (Jn 9: 2-3). There may be any number of sinful causes for the illnesses and weaknesses that beset us; addiction, abuse, violence are a few. Modern science is becoming quite good at identifying the many ways in which we destroy ourselves and our environment. Individuals and corporations contribute to the massive suffering present in the world, often in ways which are deliberate and sinful. But, that is not the immediate concern of this sarament. Rather, it is a time to consider what is to be done in terms of fruitful Christian living, given the reality of the situation as it is. Why the suffering exists is

The Sacrament of Christian Life

of major concern to the community and needs to be addressed effectively. But the sacrament of the sick is immediately concerned with alleviating the suffering that, in fact, exists and confronts us here in the subjects touched in the ritual action.

Faith assures us that God's love is neither conditioned nor limited. Faith challenges us to live fully despite conditions or limitations. This is the message to the community and to the individual. Penance is a distinct rite in which the causes of disruption can be identified and ways of overcoming them can be sought. Viaticum is the sacrament of the dying, the acceptance of the risen Lord as the guide to the fullness of life beyond death. It may be that separation of these rituals in fact as well as in understanding would be a very healthy move for the community.

Placing the ritual action of anointing within the community celebration of eucharist is a powerful way of identifying the source of the compassionate love called for in ministry to the sick. Such ministry is a specific way of being a eucharistic people, grateful for the creative power of God's love that is most evident in our weakness. The Christian people, as Jesus did in his life, need to touch and speak with the ailing members, not avoiding but entering into their situations of suffering. A community setting also brings out the wide reaching effects of suffering and allows the strength of the ritual action to flow into the lives of the family, friends, and caretakers. The frustration and helplessness of those who love and care for an ailing or aging family member call forth the ministry of compassionate love in a very special way. The

Mary Peter McGinty

community celebration of the ritual of anointing makes the members aware of those in their midst who are in need of their care and concern; it also alerts the suffering members to the depth of love which surrounds them and appreciates their presence. The ritual thus strengthens the possibility for this community to actually be body of Christ, sacrament of his presence, in their daily ministry to one another.

SACRAMENTS OF MINISTRY

IN IDENTIFYING the church as the people of God, as the body of Christ, the documents of Vatican II have given us a fresh look at the whole question of ministry within the church and of the church to the wider world. The documents identify both the nature of the Church: "the Church, in Christ, is in the nature of sacrament — a sign and instrument, that is, of communion with God and of unity among all men" (LG 1); and its mission: the Church "receives the mission of proclaiming and establishing among all peoples the kingdom of Christ and of God, and she is, on earth, the seed and the beginning of that kingdom" (LG 5). The responsibility for the life and activity of the Christian community rests with the whole people, who are the church, "established by Christ as a communion of life, love and truth, it is taken up by him also as the instrument for the salvation of all . . . it is sent forth into the whole world" (LG 9). Ministry involves any kind of service rendered to members of the faith community or to the larger world community. And the commitment to service, or ministry, is assumed in the initiation rites when an individual enters the community of faith. In baptism, Christians are ordained and consecrated to carry out the mission of Jesus in the community and in the world. In eucharist, Christians are sent forth to be the presence of divine love in the events of daily life. Serving others is a basic characteristic of the Christian way of life. Ministry is a shared responsibility which takes on a variety of forms in Christian life and tradition.

In the Christian context, Jesus is recognized as the one priest. He makes present in human history the full reality of divine love, and effectively expresses to the Father the eucharistic response of the believing community. He is the mediator of the new convenant between God and humanity; he is the source of union and of life. This presence and mission is carried on in history by the community of believers, the Church, who are committed to be the body of Christ for the world. Two basic forms of ministry have emerged in Christian tradition, embracing the diversity of service and leadership called for by the life of the body: the ministry based on baptismal commitment and the ministry designated in the sacrament of orders. As Vatican II so clearly states: "Though they differ essentially and not only in degree, the common priesthood of the faithful and the ministerial or hierarchical priesthood are none the less ordered one to another; each in its own proper way shares in the one priesthood of Christ" (LG 10). Both are crucial to the well-being of the whole body, enabling it to be an effective sacrament of Jesus risen.

In such a context, it becomes clear that the vitality of the body depends in large measure on the willingness of the members to serve the needs of the community and nourish its life. Insofar as all the members are functioning well and contributing to the overall health of the whole will the life of the body be vigorous. Only then can the Church fulfill its mis-

The Sacrament of Christian Life

sion to animate the world with the spirit of Christ, to be witnesses to Christ in all circumstances and at the very heart of the community of mankind (GS 43).

Concept of Ministry

In the early days of the Christian community, it was very clear that the members bore a solemn responsibility for the vitality of the body. They contributed according to their abilities and gifts. Some offered their homes for the assembly; some cared for the sick, the widows, and the orphans; some shared their abundance with those who had very little; some served as leaders, some as organizers, some as witnesses to the wider society. When the community assembled, each member had a sense of being a needed part of the body — whether a foot or an eye or a brain or an arm. "There is a variety of gifts but always the same Spirit; there are all sorts of service to be done, but always to the same Lord; working in all sorts of different ways in different people, it is the same God who is working in all of them. The particular way in which the Spirit is given to each person is for a good purpose" (I Co 12: 4-7). There was a genuine sense of ministry: a gift of self to and for others. This is, of course, a somewhat idealized picture of communities that were as basically human as those of today. Paul admonished the first Christians: "I cannot say that you have done well in holding meetings that do you more harm than good . . . there are separate factions among you . . . one person goes hungry while another is getting drunk" (I Co 11: 17-18, 22). It was not, and is not, easy for Chris-

113

tians to put aside their own wants and comforts to concern themselves first for the needs of others. Jesus, and after him his disciples, had to remind the people to be sensitive and responsive to each person's needs. This was the way to let God's love permeate the lives of the community. While Paul chastised the early Christians for their lapses in loving concern for one another, he encouraged them to continue to make each moment a Christ experience, in praise of God and in support of each other. "Whatever you eat, whatever you drink, whatever you do at all, do it for the glory of God. Never do anything offensive to anyone" (I Co 10: 31-32). Paul understood that the baptismal commitment ordains Christians for a life of service within the community, and for participation in the mission of the body to and for the world.

Vatican II identifies the commission of the laity as coming from the Lord himself in the actions of baptism and confirmation. "The apostolate of the laity is a sharing in the salvific mission of the Church. Through Baptism and Confirmation all are appointed to this apostolate by the Lord himself . . . to make the Church present and fruitful. . . . Thus, every lay person, through those gifts given to him, is at once the witness and the living instrument of the mission of the Church itself" (LG 33). Ministry is not a calling for a special few, nor is it a delegation from those in authority. It is a right and a privilege and a responsibility inherent in the baptismal covenant made between the Christian community and the individual. It is a privilege that belongs to absolutely every

The Sacrament of Christian Life

Christian, to be exercised in every aspect of life in human society. In addition to this, some lay persons may be called to cooperate in the specific ministry of the bishop: "Besides this apostolate which belongs to absolutely every Christian, the laity can be called in different ways to more immediate cooperation in the apostolate of the hierarchy. . . . They have, moreover, the capacity of being appointed by the hierarchy to some ecclesiastical offices" (LG 33).

Mission to the World

To live Christian life as Father-centered and other-centered people means to be concerned for and involved in the ongoing life of the community and of the whole world of God's people. Once committed to the way of life of Jesus, Christians cannot ignore or avoid the specifics of that mission that are part of their daily life. Every part of life — family, work, relaxation, successes, difficulties — is the context for ministry. Within the ordinary circumstances of the world, Christians minister to the needs of the body and of the larger society in which they live, by their presence, by their words, by their actions. Nothing falls outside this realm of influence. It is their task, as disciples of Jesus, to seek justice in their dealings with others, whether it be in the family circle or in an international conference; to help others to achieve their potential, whether that other be friend, co-worker, or emerging nation; to value and promote peace through respect for difference and reconciliation of conflicts at home, at work, in the neighborhood, and in world affairs. They should seek to be competent in their field, using their gifts to be an effective voice that will be heard. But they should also be a sacramental presence of the compassionate God who cares deeply for each person, and especially for the powerless: "It is precisely the parts of the body that seem to be the weakest which are the indispensable ones" (1 Co 12:22). In this way, they can begin to bring the spirit of Christ into active participation in the complex societies of the modern world with all their cultural diversity and technological skill. The love of God can touch and make a difference only when it is embodied through the persons who know that love. That is the mission of Jesus: that everyone may know the love of the Father. For this, is each Christian ordained at baptism; to be the embodiment of that mission. Each one is sent forth to be a sacramental presence of faithful love.

Ministry within the Christian community takes many forms, depending on the talents of the individual and the present needs of a specific community. Ideally, each community can identify its needs and call upon those members who are most suited to alleviate them. Members of the community are not to be passive followers, but responsible participants in the life of the local church. Each can contribute specific skills: counselling, carpentry, teaching, organizing, accounting, public speaking, painting, visiting, reconciling, entertaining. For, ministry deals with every aspect of the lives of the members of the community. Wherever there is need, the concern

The Sacrament of Christian Life

of the community should be present. Christians are meant to be an embodiment of the risen Jesus, to allow his presence to touch the lives of people here and now.

The mission of the community itself to the world is to show forth the message of the resurrection to everyone: more life is a real possibility. Is the opening up of life through education a possibility for the poor and the powerless? Yes, when people care enough to make it happen. Can the violence and despair of the drug scene be turned around into a possibility for productive living? Yes, when people care enough to make it happen. Is there a real possibility of a future for the abandoned and abused children of society? Yes, when people care enough to make it happen. Can the greed for wealth and power which underlies so much of the hostility in the world be converted into a zeal for the improvement of human life? Yes, when people care enough to make it happen. The baptismal commitment proclaims a resolve to make the possibilities for life come to fruition. It is a resolve to care as Jesus cares, to love as God loves; to be a sacramental presence that is effective. The gospels give us a picture of how Jesus served the people he encountered in his life among us. He taught the multitudes, he instructed his disciples, he fed them when they were hungry, he comforted them when they suffered the loss of a child, he prayed for them, he feasted with them, he cared for the sick, he drew them to the Father and let them know of the Father's love for them. He ministered to them. Christians are called to be this pres-

117

ence for the people they live amongst and encounter throughout the day. This mission of Jesus is the responsibility of every one who is baptized in his name.

Leadership Ministry

Within the local churches, and uniting them as one universal church, there are ministers who serve in the specific areas of leadership and worship. In the rites of ordination, they are called forth from the community to be a visible presence of the risen Lord, to unify the body, to mediate the love of the Father to his people, to act and speak on behalf of the whole body. From the earliest times, these leaders have been identified as bishop, presbyter, and deacon. They share in the baptismal commitment to service and witness with all Christians. Yet, the community has asked them to assume roles of specific service within the body: "the priesthood of priests, while presupposing the sacraments of initiation, is nevertheless conferred by its own particular sacrament" (PO 2). In the rituals of holy orders, they have been liturgically confirmed by the laying on of hands and the conferring of specific tasks for the community: to assemble the people, to preside at the liturgies, to proclaim the gospel message, to unify the churches, to communicate God's love to his people. They have been respected as both the embodiment of the risen Jesus within the community and the embodiment of the Christian community in its relations with the other churches and with the world community.

The Sacrament of Christian Life

The bishop is the effective leader within the local church, "each bishop having responsibility for the particular church assigned to him" (CD 3). The pastoral care of the Christian community in its daily efforts to function as the body of Christ belongs fully to the bishop: "nor are they to be regarded as vicars of the Roman Pontiff; for they exercise the power which they possess in their own right" (LG 27). His authority, and his responsibility, is exercised "personally in the name of Christ" and is "proper, ordinary and immediate" (LG 27). He is aided by those presbyters and deacons who have been specifically commissioned to support his ministry. The bishop unites the particular church with the other churches of the universal body, "each bishop represents his own Church, whereas all, together with the pope, represent the whole Church in a bond of peace, love and unity" (LG 23), and forms with the other bishops the episcopal college.

The bishop, in his consecration, is asked to assume full responsibility for the life and mission of a particular church. He is to reveal God's presence and love in this human situation, and to formalize and express the human response, especially in praise and wonder at the goodness of God. His is an official position and requires particular authorization. The universal church supplies the authority and continuity for each local church by the participation of several bishops in the consecration rites for each new bishop. Thus, the unity of faith and ministry has been maintained through the centuries and across the globe. The bishop is the one who exercises,

Mary Peter McGinty

on behalf of the community, the fullness of that priesthood which resides in Jesus alone: to mediate the divine love to all God's people and to mediate the people's loving worship to the Father. He presides at the community rituals, provides for the spiritual and temporal needs of the body, and leads in the Christian mission for peace and unity in the whole human society.

Over the years, the position of the bishop became identified with authority in the church. In the West, when the Church emerged from the Dark Ages, the bishops turned out, along with the nobility, to take charge of the development of the Christian commonwealth. As a result, their role was increasingly interpreted in legal, jurisdictional terms. Legalism made their role one of power, both jurisdictional and sacramental. Subsequently, as authority was more and more centralized in the church, the role of the bishop became that of a delegate of the Roman pontiff, conforming the local church to the decrees of the Roman church. Vatican II has again emphasized the role of the bishop as unifier and leader, as symbol of his local church. The bishop is recognized as the vicar of Christ by means of his sacramental consecration, not by the delegation of a higher authority. His communion with all the churches through union with all the bishops and the bishop of Rome is essential to the authenticity of his position. He and the other bishops, with the bishop of Rome, work together for the good of the whole Christian community as a collegial body. For this reason, Vatican II

The Sacrament of Christian Life

called for the gathering of the bishops in national councils and in universal synods on a regular basis. Each local church, and therefore each bishop, enjoys a certain autonomy in living out its Christian commitment. Yet, no church, and therefore no bishop, functions apart from the whole body of the universal church.

Each bishop is called to ministry in baptism and to specialized service in his episcopal consecration. Peter calls the bishop to consider carefully the role he has assumed: "Be the shepherds of the flock of God that is entrusted to you: watch over it, not simply as a duty but gladly, because God wants it; not for sordid money, but because you are eager to do it. Never be a dictator over any group that is put in your charge, but be an example that the whole flock can follow. When the chief shepherd appears, you will be given the crown of unfading glory" (1 P 5: 2-4). Vatican II echoes the early admonition: "In exercising his office of father and pastor the bishop should be with his people as one who serves. . . . He should so unite and mold his flock into one family that all, conscious of their duties, may live and act in the communion of charity" (CD 16). It is indeed an awesome calling, to be the presence of the high priest, Jesus, in the midst of the faithful (LG 21). The bishop in the local church and all the bishops together with the bishop of Rome are called to minister in the name of Jesus until the kingdom of peace and justice is established, "the new heavens and new earth, the place where righteousness will be at home" (2 P 3: 13).

Mary Peter McGinty

In all the ministries, particularly in the local church, the bishop relies on the assistance of the presbyters and deacons who have been ordained as public ministers for this body. They participate in the life of the local church as co-workers with the bishop, as his presence and in his name. As such, they form a collegial body with the bishop which closely mirrors the reality of the universal church — a collegial union of churches (through their bishops) with the church of Rome (the bishop of Rome, the Pope). In the earliest experience of the church, the presbyters were often a group of leaders who had been left in place to care for the needs of the community when an apostle moved on. They were the ones who saw to the day-to-day functioning of the community, resolved the difficulties, presided at the liturgical assemblies, and saw to the well-being of the members. The deacons assisted in every way, with both liturgical and practical roles. They saw to it that no member was in want and extended the ministry of the community to all. Historically, the responsibilities were more and more channeled to a single pastor in each community of Christians, with jurisdictional and sacramental powers being delegated to him by the bishop. The collegial character of the presbyterate and the role of the deacon were gradually phased out. Vatican II has called for the restoration of both. The permanent diaconate has been reinstated as a vital role in the life of the local church (LG 29). And the priests are to gather with the bishop in collegial union to work for the good of the whole body (LG 28).

The Sacrament of Christian Life

The role of the ordained ministers in the life of the Church is irreplaceable. To them is entrusted the integrity of the word proclaimed as a revelation of the risen Lord and the divine convenant. They bear the responsibility to maintain the unity of the visible body, both within the local church and as a universal communion of churches. They publicly represent the risen Lord to the believing community and take their place in the civil society as representatives of the gospel message for the world. It is an awesome ministry with unbearable responsibility: "When a man has had a great deal given him, a great deal will be demanded of him; when a man has had a great deal given him on trust, even more will be expected of him" (Lk 12: 48). The ministers rely heavily on the presence of the risen Lord and the activity of his Spirit within the community to sustain them as they seek to be faithful servants.

Variety of Ministries

The life of the church as a functioning body within the world is the responsibility of the whole body, calling for many forms of ministry. Most often, the term ministry is associated with service within the church community. This has always been and remains the most important aspect of Christian service. Too often, the ministry within the community has been left to the official ministers: bishop, priest, deacon. Fortunately, the idea of ministry has recovered its former identity with all the people of God. Everyone has some talent to share with the group. And all are called upon to be active participants in the life of the body. Some can serve in the liturgical rites of the worshipping community, as readers, acolytes, eucharistic ministers, musicians, ushers, caretakers of the altar and sacristy. Others have talents as organizers, teachers, entertainers, financial experts, builders, shoppers, or whatever. A community has so many and such varied needs that each person has some special talent which can enrich and support the corporate life. The ministry within the community is unlimited and has recently been recognized through a variety of rituals in which members are commissioned to particular service.

But, no church exists for its own sake. It is not there primarily for the good of its members, but for the mission of Jesus to the whole of God's people. It is meant to be other-centered, to go out to all the world and be the presence of God's love to all people. This is the primary mission of the local church. All members play a significant role in pursuing this ministry. For, where they are, there is the church. This body which makes the risen Jesus present in the world touches and is touched in each individual part — this eye, this ear, this foot, this arm. There is no way to touch "the church"; it is the people who form the body who can be felt and seen and heard. The mission of Jesus to the world lies in the hands of the people as they confront a particular world on a particular day. This is ministry at its most basic, and at its most effective level. It is the ministry that each Christian is called to and ordained for in the experience of bap-

The Sacrament of Christian Life

tism. Ministry means using modern technology to develop the earth in ways that make it a fitting home for the human family; it means being actively involved in various groups within society to enhance the quality of living together; it means becoming learned in the disciplines of history or mathematics or science and cultivating the arts, entering into the dialogues which identify universal values for human life. Wherever they are, Christians are committed to live in such a way that the newness of life and the power of the Spirit embraced in baptism may be evident. Through the rituals of anointing and laying on of hands, they have been ordained by the church to be the body of Christ. This they do most effectively by bringing meaning into the experience of human life.

What is most important to understand about the sacrament of orders and the complementary rites of commissioning is the fact that, as with all the sacramental rituals, the ceremony is only a beginning of what is meant to be a lifetime commitment. The ceremony initiates a process whereby Christians can pursue a calling that has attracted them to serve God, the Christian community, and the peoples of the world. A minister is not made by the laying on of hands and the consecration with oil. A minister is made through day-to-day service in response to the needs of real people. The Christian sacrament exists in the ministry actually taking place, whether it be the bishop presiding at Eucharist, the deacon feeding the poor at a shelter for the homeless, the catechist opening minds and hearts to the message of gospel love, the

125

Mary Peter McGinty

social worker rescuing a young person from disaster, the nurse providing comfort and loving care for the terminally ill, the parent struggling to understand and help a rebellious child. A Christian becomes a minister through the liturgical experience of baptism, confirmation, ordination; but most especially through the faithful participation in Eucharist and in the life and mission of the Church. The sacrament of ministry is celebrated in all the moments of Christian living.

SACRAMENTS OF INITIATION

SINCE Vatican II, it has again become evident that becoming a Christian is a life-long process going through many phases. "Incorporated into the Church by Baptism, the faithful are appointed by their baptismal character to Christian religious worship; reborn as sons of God, they must profess before men the faith they have received from God through the Church" (LG 10). Becoming a Christian involves taking on the mind of Jesus, identifying with the people who accept Jesus as Lord, and gradually developing a way of life that exemplifies the gospel message to and for the world. At times, Christians have looked upon the ritual of baptism as a one-time experience which radically changed a person: from a sinner to a saint, from an infidel to a believer, from a ward of the devil to a child of God. Pouring the water and saying the words brought about instant change. Baptism was considered to be the essential sacrament; without it there was little if any chance of entering heaven. It was viewed as an end in itself, producing its own effects.

Current thought has recaptured the original understanding of Christianity as a way of life to be pursued in the midst of everyday experience. The initiation rites begin the process involving public commitment to radical and ongoing conversion, a public identification as a disciple of Jesus, accepting a way of life with the full support of a community committed to live as the embodiment of the risen Jesus. As Peter expressed it to the early converts: ''That water [Noah's flood] is a type of the baptism which saves you now, and which is not the washing off of physical dirt but a pledge made to God from a good conscience, through the resurrection of Jesus Christ'' (1 P 3: 21). Such commitment does not produce the effect instantaneously, but initiates the process.

A Way of Life

The rite of baptism is intrinsically connected with confirmation and eucharist as the ritual of initiation into Christian life and community. The public celebration of this rite leads the individual and the community to a deeper awareness of and commitment to the process at work within their lives. From earliest times, Christians identified themselves as those who lived in the presence of the risen Lord. They understood that the way of life set out by the experience of Jesus made them different from those among whom they lived. Greed and power and pleasure were not the values emphasized by Jesus in seeking fuller human living. Herod's court was not his model for the kingdom. Rather, Jesus showed sensitivity to human needs, feeding the hungry and healing the sick. He respected and cared for persons: the taxgatherer and the fisherman, the disciple and the adulterer, the benefactor and the thief. It gradually became clear to his disciples that ''love one another as I have loved you'' was the real challenge.

The Sacrament of Christian Life

God's love is unconditional, without limit, yet demanding. To live this love in the world is to remove all class distinctions, eradicate prejudices, forego vengeance, let go of self-seeking competitiveness, curb the desire to succeed at all costs. It calls for a genuine concern for the welfare of those around us, a willingness to give time and effort to benefit others, a patience and forgiveness in dealing with the shortcomings of others, a respect for the individuality and dignity of each person, and a help to others to become what God hopes them to be: fully alive.

Incorporation of New Members

The early Christians struggled to live out this legacy to the world. It brought them many crises in a world that was dominated by power. Recognizing their commitment to be not only an identity but a way of life, they soon developed a rather elaborate process for the incorporation of new members into the community of believers. It was not enough for an individual to express a desire to be a Christian. Both the individual and the community needed time to examine the meaning of that commitment in terms of this particular person. They needed to see their lives in that context and determine what changes might be called for: in family relationships because of objections to class distinction? in employment because of conflict of values? in friendships because of unacceptable lifestyles? It would take time to sort out the real significance of a commitment to Jesus and his body, the church. At the same time, the Christian community

Mary Peter McGinty

would like to test the genuineness and sincerity of the candidate's desire to belong to the body by living in close contact with the person over an extended period of time. This period of discovery was crucial for the individual and for the community.

With a degree of satisfaction reached on both sides, the formal process of initiation could begin. The candidates were enrolled as members of the community, their names being written on the books. This was an important step, an initial commitment and identity. The candidates were now called catechumens, those who had entered into a process by which conversion could take place; a process in which they would learn of Jesus and his mission, not by didactic methods but through the experience of a believing community. The community formally participated in the preparation of the candidates through the liturgical assemblies and in the encounters of daily living.

When the individual and the community were ready to formalize this mutual commitment, the rituals of initiation were performed at the Easter vigil service. These consisted of a baptismal rite, by which the individuals entered symbolically into the death and resurrection of Christ and committed themselves to continue his mission in the world within the context of this community of faith. There followed a confirmation by the bishop, through a special anointing and laying on of hands, whereby the individuals were incorporated into the universal body with its global responsibilities and opportunities. Finally, the new members, dressed in the white

The Sacrament of Christian Life

garments of new-found innocence, were welcomed into a full participation in the eucharistic assembly, wherein they could now enjoy the fellowship of the community and draw meaning and strength for their life as Christians. This symbolized the individuals' entrance into a way of life which would be brought to fulfillment only at the moment of entry into risen life through death. It was not the end, but the beginning of a journey that would be lifelong. For the individuals, it was a commitment to a whole way of living that would encompass every moment of every day. For the community, it was a pledge of the fidelity of God's love embodied in these people who are sacrament of that love for these persons in all the experiences of daily living. For both the individuals and the community, it was a powerful experience of the meaning of Christian discipleship.

Development of the Rite

This process of initiation underwent significant changes through the centuries. The emphasis on a way of life gave way to a focus on the salvation of the individual soul. Baptism came to be looked upon as a washing away of sin and, from the time of Augustine (5th century), was connected with original sin which contaminated every soul born into this world. Entering into the death and resurrection of Jesus through the symbolic rituals of baptism was the way to salvation, since it was by his death that Christ had overcome evil and paid the price for human sin. When leaders of the Celts and of the Germanic tribes accepted salvation in Christ, they

Mary Peter McGinty

had all their subjects baptized with them. Such mass conversions left little room for an initiation process or an understanding of the impact of belief on daily life. Furthermore, Baptism became a rite in itself, separated from the confirmation by the bishop, and from the participation in the eucharistic assembly. It became an individual ceremony and *the* means of salvation. One who was baptized was freed from sin and the influence of the devil, and could be counted among the children of God. The emphasis was on going to heaven, not on living in this world and building the kingdom of God.

In the West, the separation of the rite of initiation into three sacraments was acknowledged by the twelfth century when the sacraments were numbered seven. Confirmation had been reserved for the ministry of the bishop and was therefore often delayed. Its precise meaning has been the subject of much discussion ever since. The new baptismal practice produced a new type of church: a church, not of saints but of habitual sinners, not worthy of the Eucharist because of their residual paganism. Eucharist became increasingly a kind of privileged audience with a divine king in which many considered themselves incapable of fully participating, rather than a joyful assembly of disciples who shared the experience and mission of the risen Lord. With the rise of a juridical mentality that focused on the validity of the sacraments, the correctness of the rites, and the proper jurisdiction of the ministers, there was a loss of significance for the assembly and of importance for their daily living. God's action was channeled to the people through his designated ministers by means of

The Sacrament of Christian Life

valid rites. In order to be saved, people needed to receive these sacraments in good faith and live according to God's law. Put simplistically and somewhat unfairly, law had replaced love as a sign of God's presence with his people.

Renewed Vision

Vatican II has brought back the emphasis on Christianity as a way of life, the identification of the people as the body of Christ, and the significance of the total life of the faith community. In terms of initiation into this body, the church, Vatican II called for the restoration of the process commonly used in the early church in what is called the Rite of Christian Initiation of Adults. It recognizes that being a Christian is primarily an adult experience, involving mature judgment and conscious decision. It understands the need for a nurturing community of faith if Jesus is to be known and his mission is to be adopted. "This Christian initiation, which takes place during the catechumenate, should not be left entirely to the priests and catechists, but should be the concern of the whole Christian community, especially of the sponsors, so that from the beginning the catechumens will feel that they belong to the people of God. Since the life of the Church is apostolic, the catechumens must learn to cooperate actively in the building up of the Church and in its work of evangelization, both by the example of their lives and the profession of their faith" (AG 14). The question of salvation does not depend on the reception of certain rites, but on the living out of the Christian vision in the concrete events of life. To participate in the rites of initiation involves an acceptance of God's love, a commitment to embody that love, a responsibility for and an obligation to this particular community of faith, an identification as a disciple of Jesus with a resolve to carry out his mission in and for the world. That world remains much as it was; the people around us are the same people; it is the acceptance of God's call to personal union with him and communion with his people that makes all things new.

For a Christian community, the process of initiation presents a constantly recurring experience of what it means to be a follower of Jesus. As new individuals enter into this process year after year, the whole community is confronted with its identity and mission. In attempting to explain and witness to Christian life in all its dimensions, the members of the community are faced anew with the realities of their lives. How does a businessman live his Christian commitment in the board room? Can the student recognize a responsibility to share knowledge and resources with others who are struggling to get an education? Where can Christian commitment come into play in cities which are plagued with violence, poverty, and despair? The process of initiation is a growing experience for the community no less than for the individuals involved in the rites.

In the revised rituals coming out of Vatican II, the accent once more is on the action of the whole community. The assembly of the faithful is the primary symbol of the presence of divine love. The liturgies during the season of Lent are

The Sacrament of Christian Life

specifically designated as steps in the initiation process. Here the worshipping community shares with the catechumens the reality of Christian commitment. The candidates become publicly known to the whole assembly and experience acceptance and challenge in the encounter with a community of faith. The community functions as a true sacrament, expressing in concrete terms the joy and the struggle in being body of Christ for the world.

Practical Questions

Many practical questions exist at this point in the development of these rites. If Christianity is an adult religion, why do we baptize infants and children? They can neither understand nor choose to follow the way of life proposed. If we are not trying to save them by washing away sin from their souls, what are we doing for them? It seems clear that we are sharing with them our life of faith; we are incorporating them into a community that accepts Jesus as Lord; we are introducing them to a way of life that may become consciously their own in the future. Baptism is always future-oriented, pointing the way to what can be. It is not a "done deed" which cannot be rejected. In fact, throughout history and at the present time, there are many baptized unbelievers for whom the invitation to be disciples of Jesus has remained unanswered or has been consciously rejected. There are no guarantees attached to baptism, nor are persons committed against their wills. The love of God is always an offer, an invitation. It can be accepted, rejected, or ignored. It is never forced. No baptism is completed until the moment of entry into risen life. For the infant, the community is giving of its life and its faith. The response for each person can only come in a free and mature commitment to the covenant with God. Is the infant being treated unfairly? Not if what is being offered is life and love.

Another question has to do with the meaning of confirmation. Seen within the process of initiation, it adds a dimension of belonging, of responsibility, and of public witness to the symbols of baptism. Not only does one enter into the life of this particular community of disciples of the risen Lord; one becomes incorporated into the life of the global church symbolized by the unity of this bishop with the bishops of all the particular churches throughout the world; one becomes identified with and responsible for the life of the whole body as it exists in the total world scene. No community can become closed in on itself, excluding the concerns and the needs of others. Confirmation immediately sets the new members into the full context of Christian living. It calls for a recognition of the role of the Spirit in the life of the community and that of the individuals. Learning to discern the movement of the Spirit in the events of daily life is a major part of the maturing process in Christian life; the sacramental rituals are a constant source of enlightenment and strength in this process. Confirmation also emphasizes the very reason for the existence of the church: to be an effective presence of divine love within the world for the good of the whole, to be a God-centered and other-centered people.

The Sacrament of Christian Life

When confirmation became separated from the initiation ritual, its meaning was called into question. In the West, it continued to be connected with the ministry of the bishop and, thus, frequently delayed until he could be present. The question arose as to whether the baptized person could fully participate in eucharist. Eventually, the resolution recognized the effectiveness of baptism as incorporation into the life of the community and the right of the baptized person to full membership and full participation, even though not yet confirmed by the bishop. This led to a practice which interrupted the flow of the initiation rites. Baptism became the essential sacrament which gave access to the other rites. Full participation in eucharist was eventually opened to those who had reached the age of reason. The initiation context was lost sight of, and confirmation was on its own. There have been many attempts to justify its existence as a sacrament and its position within the context of the seven. Some of these have identified it as a rite of maturity and of personal owning of the baptismal commitment assumed in infancy. The difficulties arise from the disruption of an original initiation ritual into three separated actions.

Vatican II has begun a process of seeking to restore an effective sacramental experience into the life of the community. The RCIA ritual keeps the rites together in a single initiation process. For adults, this can be a very effective introduction into the Christian life. The question of the sequence of the rituals for those baptized in infancy is still unresolved. The linking of the three rites is clearly sym-

Mary Peter McGinty

bolized, but confirmation is usually administered out of sequence and at a later age, often with the significance of maturity and personal choice. Much of the responsibility for Christian living and concern for others is identified with this sacrament of maturity, leaving baptism and eucharist somewhat in the background as rites of initiation into a way of life. At times, the preparation for the rite of confirmation can assume a somewhat pelagian appearance, with candidates being required to master certain knowledge and to perform prescribed numbers of good works in order to participate in the rite. The sense of earning God's love can be communicated in this approach. God's initiative and free gift of love can be lost sight of. It is true that young Christians need to learn to identify their particular gifts and to be guided in effective use of those gifts on behalf of others. Yet, our society tends to emphasize the concept of payment/reward for works performed. Care needs to be taken so that young Christians learn the value of doing for others without expectation of return/recompense, and most especially the unconditional character of God's love which cannot be earned, but is always freely given.

In an ideal future, the Christian community, drawing deeply from its origins and tradition, will be able to resolve these and other difficulties, and once more celebrate effective rites of initiation of new members into the life and mission of the risen Jesus.

CHALLENGES AND OPPORTUNITIES

THE WORLD we live in changes so rapidly and so dramatically that it is difficult to keep up with it. "Ours is a new age of history with critical and swift upheavals spreading gradually to all corners of the earth. They are the products of man's intelligence and creative activity, but they recoil upon him, upon his judgments and desires, both individual and collective, upon his ways of thinking and acting in regard to people and things. We are entitled then to speak of a real social and cultural transformation" (GS 4). We have seen the demise of communism as a world power, the opening up of previously isolated countries, the return of the open practice of religion to formerly atheist peoples. We are in the midst of such an explosion of technology that it overwhelms our corporate intelligence. The possibilities in our present life confront us with hitherto uncalled for decisions and responsibilities — the possibilities for travel, for communication, for information storage, retrieval, and transmission, for control of disease and of the most sensitive processes of human reproduction. At the same time, the capabilities for destruction have multiplied — nuclear power, missiles, satellites, chemical substances, computer invasion of knowledge can all be used to destroy as well as to enhance human life. "There appears the dichotomy of a world that is at once powerful and weak, capable of doing what is noble and what is base, disposed to freedom and slavery, progress and decline, brotherhood and hatred. Man is growing conscious that the forces he has unleashed are in his own hands and that it is up to him to control them or be enslaved by them'' (GS 9). For any one who has lived through the last ninety years, the world is a totally new place and earth is a much smaller planet. For any one who loved life in the sixties, the dream of Camelot has given way to the excitement and the fears of science fiction.

One thing the Christian community cannot afford to do is to become complacent or to remain stagnant. Vatican II certainly made that clear in its call for change in the liturgical life, for change in the understanding of what it means to be church, for change in the relationship with the world and the wide diversity of peoples and religions within our societies. In order to live the mission of Jesus within history, it is essential to be alert to and responsive to the events in the life of the human society in which church exists and for which it is meant to be an instrument and sign of salvation. While Christians rejoice in the renewal of religious practice in lands where it had been officially banned, they must assume the responsibility to be Christian community for and with the peoples who have had little or no experience of Christian faith. Where governments are severely oppressing large portions of their population, sometimes to the point of starvation, Christian communities can seek to be effective voices for liberation of the powerless and can find ways to alleviate their suffering by supplying food and shelter and medical

The Sacrament of Christian Life

care. Christian communities can be effective counter cultures where portions of the population in successful countries are exploiting their own people through greed, lucrative drug dealing, cutthroat competition, and media-enhanced materialism. The lives of the Christian communities can show the possibility of and the value in being other-centered: sharing resources, caring for the well-being of the other, helping another to succeed, living simply and treasuring this world and all it has to offer.

With the potential present in our world, a potential that can be used for good or for destruction, the need is increased for an attentiveness to the movement of the Spirit of God in the midst of his people, within the community of believers and within the larger community of humanity. ''The fundamental law of human perfection, and consequently of the transformation of the world, is the new commandment of love. . . . This love is not something reserved for important matters, but must be exercised above all in the ordinary circumstances of daily life. . . . Christ is now at work in the hearts of men by the power of his Spirit; not only does he arouse in them a desire for the world to come but he quickens, purifies, and strengthens the generous aspirations of mankind to make life more humane and conquer the earth for this purpose'' (GS 38).

Challenge of Pluralism

The changes which occur in society present the people of God with significant challenges. The challenge of pluralism

Mary Peter McGinty

has increased immeasurably in the recent development of a global society, with its "state of the art" advances in science and the social sciences. Foreign cultures, customs, traditions are no longer interesting material for research and reading enjoyment. They have become part of the everyday experience of all but the most isolated of peoples. The security of being surrounded by persons who share a world vision and a practical set of values for living in this world is a thing of the past. Instead, people now find themselves living next door to persons of different nationality, race, religious belief, or cultural traditions. Simple communication often demands a great deal of patience and tolerance. It also requires intelligent reflection on the basis for one's own beliefs and values.

Even within the community of Christian believers, there is a dramatic increase in pluralism. The sixteenth century saw a practical challenge to many practices and dogmatic statements which brought about division within Christianity. The growth of nationalism was already dividing Western society. Anticlericalism and disrespect for papal authority were increasing. The distance between God and the people reached alarming proportions, with fear and the necessity to earn salvation replacing a covenant of creative love. A variety of Christian churches began to appear, each emphasizing a particular way of salvation, whether by surrender to the grace of God or by faith in God's will to save all or by adherence to the teachings of the Scriptures. The disagreements have multiplied throughout the centuries, disrupting

The Sacrament of Christian Life

the one communion in the Lord's supper, until the one body of Christ now exists within over two thousand entities.

But an even greater challenge faces the Christian churches in today's movement toward a global society. No longer can Christianity be identified as a phenomenon of Western culture to be exported intact to other cultures. The Christian church of today is assuming a new face, or more accurately, new faces. The Christian church as it has been identified throughout the history of Western civilization exists in today's world as a minority of the Christian community. The church is emerging within the cultures of Africa, Asia, and Latin America at a rapid pace and with an intensity of life that has already surpassed the Western experience of Christian life. It has become in very concrete terms a universal church, a communion of particular churches. So much variety in terms of customs and traditions, as well as of intellectual expression, presents a stunning challenge to the Western church and, most especially, to the leaders of the universal church in Rome.

Challenge of Rapid Change

The rapidity of change in our global society poses its own problems. For one thing, stability is beyond the experience of a large portion of the population. What was taken for granted yesterday does not exist today. Travel, communications, scientific progress, historical discoveries are presenting challenges to long-held beliefs and practices and are opening up new approaches to values and lifestyles. Societies that were formerly self-enclosed are feeling the pressure from within as their people rub shoulders with more liberal societies in universities, business ventures, world peace endeavors and lucrative tourist trade. Scientific advances in the realms of human reproduction, management of the dying process, genetic cure of disease have faced the entire human community with intolerable burdens of decisions and choices. Evidence of the deterioration of planet Earth in many ways that are vital to human life has brought the world community to a realization of it limits and its responsibilities. When the earth itself is seen as vulnerable and the entire human race is subject to easy annihilation, there is little sense of stability left. Within this context, the Christian churches themselves have undergone radical change in the past decades, leading some people to wonder if even God can be counted on any more. What to believe, what is acceptable, what really matters are frequent questions which eat away at the firmness of faith commitment.

Challenge to Community

One of the most severe challenges presented by both pluralism and rapid change is the threat to community. A mobile society has sorely strained the security of family, of neighborhood, of faith community. Children frequently do not stay in one school or home long enough to form friendships that will last. An older generation may continue, at age

The Sacrament of Christian Life

seventy, to meet yearly within their kindergarten chums. They grew up together through thirteen years of local schooling and have remained close through all the years. What is the future for a child of today who has shared no more than two years with any other, who constantly needs to adjust to new schools, new houses, new neighbors, new areas to explore. It is a different existence which does not encourage strong involvement or close bonds. Add to this the disruption of family life through separation and divorce, the distancing from the extended family of grandparents, uncles and aunts and cousins. For many children, the risk of becoming attached to another person is just too great. A certain reserve builds up, not only in children, when the stability and security within a society is threatened. And community, which is the basis for church, becomes more difficult to achieve.

Temptations of Progress

As an individual's ties with people have become more tenuous, scientific and technological advances have brought new kinds of temptation into human society. The marvels of the universe and of human abilities are beginning to outpace the concern for others and the sense of responsibility which mark a humane and Christian society. Competition and control can become dominant attitudes within human relationships. It is better to win than to lose, it is better to have more than to have less, it is better to be on top of the heap than on the bottom. Possession of material goods gives a sense of superiority, of wealth and power and prestige. Need is replaced by craving, and limits are set aside along with responsibility for the common good. Whatever hinders, or is thought to hinder, the pleasure of possession must be eliminated. Thus, couples choose not to have children, not only out of worry or fear, but also out of a plain resolve to enjoy more luxury as well as the time to pursue their own interests. Children who are conceived are brought to full term only if they are scientifically proven to be healthy, intelligent, and of the preferred sex. In a highly competitive society, there is less and less room for any form of weakness or dependence. Human ingenuity is being put to work to build a better world. The question to be asked: is it building the kingdom?

The Positive Picture

That is not to say that the picture is entirely bleak, with little or no hope. The spirit of God is among us! The love of God does not control human existence, but it is a powerful invitation to life. The challenges of contemporary society are also the opportunities for growth and development. They present a call for the Christian community to open its eyes and enter into the midst of everyday concerns in all parts of the world. The body of Christ is a living organism and therefore subject to constant and demanding change. It needs to adapt and respond to whatever is happening at the moment, with all the knowledge and wisdom gained through previous experience and with all the creativity and ingenuity available in the spirit-filled members of the body.

The Sacrament of Christian Life

Opportunities in Pluralism

Pluralism has opened up many new avenues for Christian understanding. For one thing, it has brought home to the Christian people the universality of our God; he is not exclusively a Christian God, but the creator and savior of every human person and of the entire universe. Peoples of other faiths are not to be seen as enemies or as pagans who worship false gods. They belong to the people of God and are dearly loved members of the human family. The experience of pluralism has also prodded the Christian people to come to terms with their own identity. What do they believe and why? What makes their faith and practice different from others? When they cannot count on everyone in the society to share their understanding and their expression of values, what is the basis for their own way of life? The result of such reflection can be a much stronger sense of what it means to be a disciple of Jesus and what is involved in living the gospel message as a deliberate commitment. It is not just that people go to different churches on Sunday; it is a question of how they confront the decisions and struggles of every day that really expresses their belief in God and their hope for humanity. This is where they can truly be sacrament of the love of God, effective in and for the life of the world.

Opportunities in Change

The rapidity of change and the experience of instability present an opportunity for realizing the ''not-yet'' of earthly existence. Creation of a world and a people is a task that continues to call forth the best efforts of all human beings to become what they can be. God is fully present and active in the process of creation. He invites all persons to function as free agents in pursuing the goals of a better world and full human living. Our own experience confirms the unfinished state of the creative process. The longer we live, the more we realize that we have not yet "arrived." We never seem to reach that "permanent resting place," but always sense the need to move on. Our Christian faith awakens us to the excitement of a life that is open to being more than it is. Our belief in resurrection, realized in Jesus, gives us the certainty that the goal can be achieved. The opportunity is before us as a very real possibility.

Opportunities for Faith Community

The threats to community presented by modern society can also be seen as opportunities for faith. Sooner or later, we may ask ourselves what it is that makes a community. What is important for true and lasting relationships? What can bind a people together in the face of difficult situations? Are things and success the real measure of the worth of a human person? Sooner or later, the reality of our oneness as God's people may hit home. Faith tells us that it is God's love that unites us as one people. Faith tells us that we are one body in Christ. No other tie can have the strength and endurance of that bond. Experience may lead us to that realization and begin to draw us together. A community thus formed becomes

The Sacrament of Christian Life

a powerful force in the society, as the earliest Christian communities were. Such a community becomes a sacrament of God's love, effectively carrying out the mission of Jesus in all parts of human life.

The challenge and the opportunity are clear. Christians are challenged to be what they say they are: the body of Christ. They are to be in this world what Jesus was in his human life among us: the revelation of the love of God for all his people and the revelation of the ultimate meaning of human life. Jesus did not change the political or religious leaders of his time. He did have an effect on the lives of people who lived in the conditions of the time. The operating force was always love. God loves unconditionally; the poor and the rich, the good and the bad, the powerful and the weak. He asks that we love as he does, without preference or prejudice, without self-seeking or privilege, without excluding anyone. That is what it means to be body of Jesus, to be sacrament of love.

Rituals for Life

The actions of the Christian community identified as sacraments are meant to focus the attention of the believers on this task and this mission. Eucharist and marriage deal with the all-the-time process of daily living; the ordinary happenings that tend to lose their significance, the conflicts and crises that drain away strength, the joys and successes that may lead to self-complacency. Reconciliation and anointing bring us face to face with the limitations of human living; the need for wholeness in a body corrupted by sin and self-centeredness, the need for the support of the whole body when a member is weakened by old age or illness. The conferring of ministries on members of the community recalls the interdependence of all and the need to serve the well-being of the body; those who are called to serve in specific ways should be supported in carrying out that ministry, and all should stand ready to nourish the life of the body in whatever way they can. The initiation rituals are particularly significant in renewing the identity of the community and its commitment to the mission of Jesus; to experience once again what it means to be a Christian and how that is to be lived out in today's society in this particular place.

A Life of Love

The body of Christ is a living organism, responding to and effectively living within a particular society. It is crucial that it be (1) a living organism, (2) living within a particular society, (3) as an expression of God's initiative of love. A body is at once diverse and unified. The community of believers who are drawn together as disciples of the risen Jesus are at once many and one. It is this sense of community, or peoplehood, of interdependent belonging that is perhaps most lacking in the experience of church today. The secular society does not do much to foster this type of bonding, but rather works against it in many ways. American society, in particular, with its emphasis on the individual may downplay the idea of dependence. Yet, the parts of a body have no

The Sacrament of Christian Life

meaning or function apart from the organism. To maintain a uniqueness while being submerged in a whole is characteristic of Christian identity and, in fact, of human identity. It is the sense of wholeness that seems to elude us at the present. Many Christian churches are wrestling with this question of becoming a true community without surrendering the independence of the individual. It is becoming evident that communities need to be smaller and, perhaps, to be gathered together in some way other than geographical location. At the same time, it is essential to maintain the diversity of the group, so that churches do not break into factions or disparate groups. In large cities, the need is greatest: to avoid anonymity and bring together communities who truly share faith and life, who are one in Christ. Small communities (family, neighbors, co-workers) are needed who share the sacramental experience of eucharist, marriage, reconciliation, anointing, ministry in their daily living, and can identify their own effectiveness in making the love of God present in specific instances of their lives. There is a pressing need to make this awareness concrete and common, to help Christians identify themselves as body, as sacrament. This small community needs to come together with other small communities to broaden the experience and the awareness of Jesus' mission. What is being called for is a re-examination of the structure of church as growing from the small to the larger, rather than as divided from the whole into parts. Crucial to the life of the whole and to the integrity of any part is the union in Christ.

Mary Peter McGinty

Commitment to Christ, explicit in the initiation rituals, is the life source of the body and the only bond strong enough to maintain its unity.

As body of Christ, this community cannot exist for its own benefit. Jesus had one purpose in living: that they may know the one true God. His way of making God known was by being a living embodiment of who God is. It is that task that falls to his body, the people who decisively choose to live his way. That task takes this people into the highways and byways of the world. They cannot remain secure within their own enclaves, nor venture forth only into comfortable settings. The love of God is universal, embracing every person in every place at every time. The body of Jesus is in this world in order to make that love known. How? As Jesus did. The challenge is to be that kind of love in any and every situation, with any and every person in the ordinary course of a day. That is to be sacrament of God's love. The response to the expression of love may be positive; it may be rejection. What is important is that the love be felt, and that it be consistent. The Christian community needs to maintain its strength and its authenticity by frequent gatherings and ritual experience of who God is for us in Jesus. But the sacramentality of their lives operates at an effective level in the ordinary setting of home and workplace, ballpark and restaurant, streets and alleys. Once this concept of Christian commitment is grasped, the community of church begins to come alive.

With our tendency to self-reliance and our admiration of

The Sacrament of Christian Life

an independent spirit, we may lose sight of the role of God in our lives and in all of creation. Faith tells us that the whole of the universe exists as a result of God's initiative of love. Both words are important. God made the first move and continues to do so. He began the process of creation as an expression of his love and as an invitation to become a world and a people growing towards a fullness of life in harmony. Love such as God is does not wait to be asked, does not act in response, does not delay until conditions are right. Love is a constant and consistent offer and invitation: an offer of self-gift and an invitation to union. That initiative on God's part is always present in every situation of life. Since it is an initiative of love, it is not there to control, to manipulate, to exploit, to reward or punish. It is there as an aid and as a stimulus. It is the real possibility within each moment; it is the assurance of acceptance even in the midst of seeming failure. The danger is that we get so caught up in our need to achieve, to steer events in the right direction, to alleviate the suffering we encounter that we may forget the power of the love of God which is available to bring forth the full possibilities of the moment. We may forget that as Christian community, as Christian individuals, we are the body of Jesus. As such, we are committed to make the Father's love effective wherever we are. To do that, we have to allow that love to be embodied in us and thus to touch the persons and the world. This is the process of transformation that can truly be called sacramental.

What we are saying becomes rather simple. The sacrament

of God's love is Jesus in his human living amongst us, in Palestine long ago and in risen life in our midst today. The body of Jesus, making him present in our world, is the Christian community of disciples who have committed themselves to be this presence in today's society. These assembled disciples become body of Jesus in and through the action of eucharist where they are constantly challenged to pursue the mission of Jesus: to praise the Father and to make the Father known. The rituals of the assembled community of Christians have as their goal to sustain and invigorate the sacramental living where love can be expressed and transformation can take place. It is this which we identify as the sacrament of Christian life.